HIDDEN HISTORY *of* BURLINGTON VERMONT

HIDDEN HISTORY *of* BURLINGTON VERMONT

Glenn Fay Jr.

Foreword by Melinda Moulton,
CEO, Main Street Landing

Published by The History Press
Charleston, SC
www.historypress.com

Front cover: Silver Special Collections, UVM.
Back cover, top: reconstruction by Kevin Crisman; *bottom*: courtesy of the author.

First published 2022

Manufactured in the United States

ISBN 9781467152105

Library of Congress Control Number: 2022931444

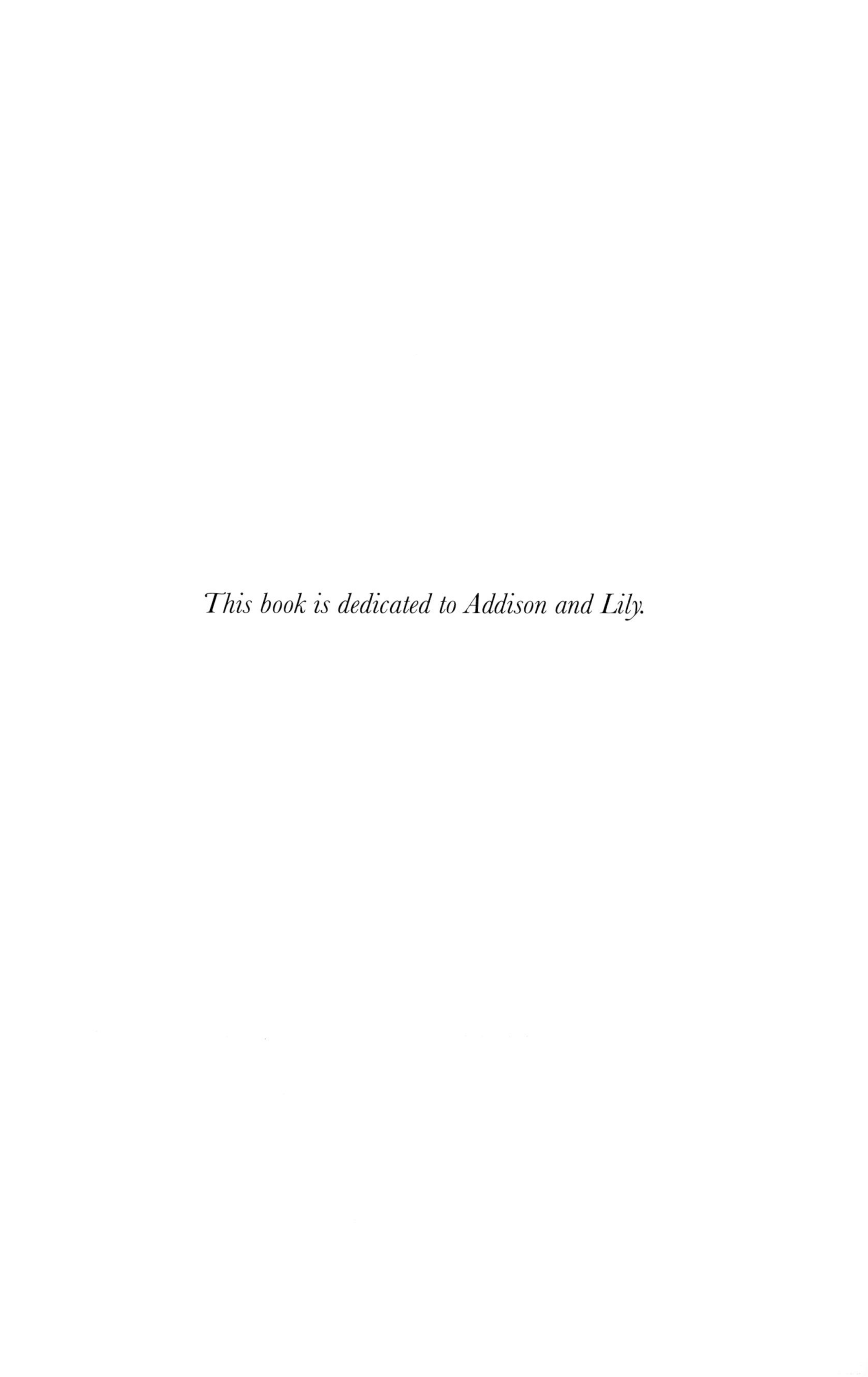

This book is dedicated to Addison and Lily.

Contents

Foreword

Having been a cofounder and CEO of Main Street Landing, I have played a role in the forty-year transformation of the built environment that lies to the east of the shores of Lake Champlain in downtown Burlington, Vermont. In this capacity, we endeavored to transform the central waterfront area from an old industrial site into a healthy, accessible and affordable center for events, retail, recreation and office space where people can work, play, live and thrive. The history of Burlington has been an important context to inform our planning, and it drove our vision in almost everything we accomplished.

In my work on various boards in the city and state, I have been fortunate to work with many people who value those characters who came before us and the values that went into making and keeping Burlington a great place to live, work and thrive. In his book *Hidden History of Burlington, Vermont*, Glenn Fay has dug deep into the real-life characters, events and structures that influence who we are today.

Whether you are a general reader or a seasoned historian, a native Burlingtonian or a visitor, you will appreciate this book. Fay carefully unravels the complexities of life in the 1700s, 1800s and early 1900s as Burlington evolved from wilderness into a town and, finally, a city. He takes us into the personal stories of some of the founders and prominent citizens, visitors, events, triumphs and hardships during the ups and downs of time.

Burlington has created and hosted a long list of world-class celebrities and leaders. One of the most interesting visitors appeared in February 1793.

His Excellency Prince Edward, Duke of Kent and Strathearn, and his lady friend Madame de Saint-Laurent, stayed at the home of Phineas Loomis for a couple of nights. Loomis ran a successful hillside tannery and leather shop on what would become known as Pearl Street. His home was the largest accommodation for the entourage, including the royal military escort, attendants, chef, food, several sleighs of carryalls and bodyguards, who slept by his door. The prince was a son of King George III, King of Great Britain. Of course, America had defeated the king's army in the Revolutionary War in 1783. Later, the prince would father Queen Victoria.

Eye-catching architecture is one of the first things visitors notice in Burlington, and everyone has their favorites. A handful of spectacular nineteenth-century buildings carry histories that are as interesting as the design and craftsmanship. Many people know that Grasse Mount was owned by Governor Cornelius Van Ness and that he hosted the Marquis de Lafayette. But the carved white marble fireplaces, hand-painted trompe l'oeil walls, stenciled ceilings, black walnut and curly maple woodwork and jeweled window treatments are jaw-dropping.

The Edward Wells house that sits next door, with curved, clear and stained glass in a round turret, extensive wood carving by Albert Whittekind and Queen Anne–style grandeur, is a masterpiece. UVM's Old Mill, with its towering Tiffany stained-glass arched windows and pointed-steeple bell tower, is a must-see and today serves as the university logo. When the gold dome was replaced with the newer pointed bell tower in 1884, faculty and students ridiculed it for decades. But many people think Billings Library is the architectural gem of campus, and for good reasons. Visitors will find unique aspects of the exterior design, such as the Syrian arch, round and polygonal turrets and carved sandstone. Inside is a grand space of apses, cathedral ceilings, exposed beams and hammerbeam trusses.

Of the three hundred shipwrecks that lie in Lake Champlain, three of them are in Burlington Bay. One vessel is a sixty-three-foot-long horse ferry, a paddle wheeler that was powered by two trotting horses on a wood turntable. These were common ferryboats for a few decades on the lake. A couple of gaff-rigged canal boats also sit on the bottom of the bay. Both of them succumbed to vicious storms. Another interesting boat—not submerged—was the William Randolph Hearst personal yacht *Oneida*, which was purchased by a colorful Lake Champlain ship captain. He repurposed the *Oneida* as a passenger and car ferry and as a museum that operated for some time in the early twentieth century.

Several churches have burned in Burlington, including the First Congregational Church, which was built in 1812; a rare image of that white clapboard church in this book tells a story. Those of us who lived in Burlington in the 1970s will remember the string of arsons and electrical fires that claimed two iconic cathedrals built in the 1830s: St. Paul's Episcopal Cathedral and the Cathedral of the Immaculate Conception. Both were architectural beauties and powerful cultural centers for 140 years.

Fay also explores the emergence of distinct neighborhoods over time, as new Americans helped build the city, from the East End river mills to the waterfront, to the Old North End, to the South End, as well as the interesting histories of three early parks. Burlington's twists and turns are echoes of the past that remind us we can learn from it and take stock in what we have today.

This book hints at our strong sense of place, our resilience and the reason Burlington rises to the top of so many "greatest places to live" lists.

—Melinda Moulton
CEO, Main Street Landing
Burlington, Vermont

Acknowledgements

Burlington residents enjoy a strong sense of place and a powerful appreciation for their history. But historical artifacts and records would not exist without extensive repositories collected from the past. The historians and historical organizations that preserve and collect artifacts deserve our credit and support. Many organizations are run by volunteer individuals who generously give their time and go out of their way to bring the past to light. The Chittenden County Historical Society and the Ethan Allen Homestead Museum are two local organizations that are run by volunteers who keep history alive and support research and education through their activities. Thank you to these organizations and all of the people who generously supported this project, in particular Dan O'Neil, the former executive director of the Ethan Allen Homestead Museum. Thank you to Dr. Fred Wiseman and Patrick Lamphear of the Vermont Indigenous Heritage Center for their consultation.

Other organizations, such as the Vermont State Archives, the Fletcher Free Library, the University of Vermont libraries, the Vermont Historical Society, the Library of Congress and the National Archives, have accumulated vast collections of artifacts and records that are curated by professionals. Thank you to all of these organizations for preserving history and for their help in my research.

Two legendary Burlington historians, David Blow and Vincent Feeney, have devoted years of scholarship to exploring and unraveling the history of Burlington and the people who have lived here before us. Both of these men have authored books on Burlington history, and this book wouldn't be the same without their scholarship. Bob Blanchard, another generous local historian and founder of the *Burlington Area History* blog, is an indefatigable source of history as well. Thank you to Joseph Perron, Jason Stuffle and many other Burlington historians who share material with the community. Thank you to Prudence Doherty and the accommodating staff at the University of Vermont (UVM) Special Collections Library for their expert help in ferreting out golden nuggets from the archives. Thank you UVM historian Thomas Visser and his students for many years of research projects on the old buildings and neighborhoods in Burlington.

Thank you to Jeff Potash for his help in unraveling aspects of the early Jewish community. Thank you to Old East End historian David Cawley for his generous help. A special thanks to Kevin Crisman, nautical archaeologist at Texas A&M, Art Cohn and Patricia Reid and others at the Lake Champlain Maritime Museum. Thank you, Howard Lincoln at the UVM Foundation, for the tour of the Wells House and Grasse Mount.

Finding historic images of people and places before the era of photography is always a challenge, and pictures often speak a thousand words. Thank you, Laura Hollowell at the Lake Champlain Basin Program, and Julie Eldridge Edwards, curator of collections at Shelburne Farms. Thanks also goes to the First Congregational Church, which found a rare sketch of its first building, which burned in 1839. I sincerely appreciate the help of Lisa DeNatale from the Vermont Italian Cultural Association. She went out of her way to chase down images and obtain permission for me to use them. As a result, thank you to Assistant Archivist Kathleen Messier at the Roman Catholic Diocese and Louis Izzo for the use of their images.

Thanks goes to Christine Auer Hebert and Joan Bromley for the opportunity to chat and listen to their insights and stories about the past. Thank you, Melinda Moulton at Main Street Landing, for your environmentally conscious leadership for the public good and encouragement for this project. Thank you, Mike Kinsella, Rick Delaney and the other editors at Arcadia Publishing/The History Press. Thank you, Suzanne, for your insight on Burlington architecture and craftsmanship. Finally, thank you to my wife, Donna, whose common sense and support sustained my work.

Introduction

When I began this project, it seemed that it would be easy. What history buff wouldn't want to write a book about their hometown, a place rich with stories and stature that wins accolades on a regular basis? But during my research, as the years rolled back and the colorful characters from the past emerged, too many intriguing paths and people presented themselves. A small city with so many spectacular achievements, monuments and dramas has endless stories to tell—probably too many to adequately narrate within the constraints of a couple hundred pages and forty images.

The challenge became how to select the essential, most intriguing stories and photos within the parameters of time and space. Chronologically, the story begins with the eons of geology that left an indelible context on so much of Burlington's past and present. And the endpoint of this book becomes the chronological boundary of the living memory of those of us who are alive today, which is perhaps the 1920s.

Therefore, except for urban renewal and the dramatic cathedral fires, this book stops short of our own personal memories. Those old stories are reserved for another author and another time. Sadly, many colorful images, particularly the stunning Old Mill Tiffany stained glass and Grasse Mount artisan work, could not be included in this black-and-white book. They are posted on the Hidden History of Burlington page online for readers to enjoy.

This book does not take the reader on a chronological walk through time. Instead, it unravels intriguing tales and images of older times with humble beginnings and some not-so-humble outcomes. It illuminates some of the more interesting characters, origins, fortunes and follies. It highlights architectural spectacles, the emergence of distinct neighborhoods and, finally, some dramatic events and big changes leading up to the middle of the twentieth century. These stories echo the ebb and flow of the hidden history of Burlington.

I

IT TAKES ALL KINDS

1
The Royal Treatment

It was a cold night in February 1789. One of Vermont's legendary founders, General Ethan Allen, had just passed away and left his widow, Fanny Allen, and young children, living in their frame house near the Winooski River in Burlington, Vermont. Allen had been heading home across the ice of Lake Champlain after spending the night at his cousin Ebenezer Allen's tavern on the island of South Hero, fifteen miles away. The American Revolution had ended six years earlier.

At about the same time in 1789, an enterprising man named Phineas Loomis was moving his family northward from Allen's former hometown in Sheffield, Massachusetts. Loomis was headed to the land of opportunity, an up-and-coming town called Burlington in the independent republic of Vermont. The family made it as far as Benson, and at that point, the road north dwindled to a narrow path. He then took to the ice on Lake Champlain and traveled the rest of the way near the shoreline. Once he arrived in Burlington, Loomis found a thick oak and pine forest on a hillside overlooking the pristine lake and New York State mountains.

Burlington barely had three hundred inhabitants scattered through its 35,000 acres, living in log cabins and small frame homes. The Onion (Winooski) River meandered along the north edge of the town and offered water power for mills, which were essential to saw logs into lumber and grind wheat into flour. Loomis bought 20 hillside acres and moved his family into a log cabin on the property at the west corner of what would become Pearl Street and South Williams Street. The following year, with the help of neighbors, he erected a large frame home on the property—the biggest house in town.

Lake Street, which is now called Battery Street, bordering the edge of the lake at that time, was only a path that turned east onto another path that would become Pearl Street, which extended up to the top of the hill (now Colchester Avenue), then curved left down to a settlement at the falls. Across the river was the town of Colchester (now Winooski). By 1790, Loomis had built a successful leather tannery, which was a lucrative business for the fur trade. Beaver, deer, cattle and other plentiful mammals provided raw material for tanneries.

The small town was booming, with newcomers arriving every week. Properties changed hands without town land records until 1798. And early on, most of the property was owned by Vermont founder Ira Allen and his brothers. Settlers moved in and cleared their acreage for timber and farming. Cows, pigs and other livestock wandered off their farms into the muddy paths and roads. Businesses opened for trade, barter and promissory notes. The population would triple in the next ten years. But something momentous would happen to Phineas Loomis in 1793 that no one could have predicted.

In February 1793, four years after he had arrived in Burlington, Phineas Loomis, who had the biggest and most comfortable house in town, enjoyed the privilege of entertaining some of the foremost celebrities in the world: King George III's twenty-eight-year old son, His Royal Highness Prince Edward Augustus, Duke of Kent and Strathearn, and his "mistress," Madame Alphonsine-Thérèse-Bernardine-Julie de Montgenêt de Saint-Laurent. The "mistress," as she was called at the time, was a girlfriend to the bachelor prince and not a mistress in the sense of the word we use today. Nonetheless, the visit was more than a big deal in the tiny town of Burlington; this was "a happenin'!"

Remember, many American Patriots despised King George III, the notorious ruler of the United Kingdom and architect of the British army and navy, one of the mightiest militaries in the world, if not the best. The British had lost the Revolution to General George Washington and the American colonial army and militias, with a bit of help from France. King George III was widely seen as a mentally ill tyrant and often blamed for the British losing the war.

The king had banished Prince Edward to Gibraltar, later Halifax, then Quebec City, because George was fed up with Edward's less-than-noble taste in women. The king was especially disconcerted with Prince Edward's illicit relationship with Madame de Saint-Laurent, who wasn't endowed

Left: Prince Edward Augustus, Duke of Kent and Strathearn. *Right*: Madame de Saint-Laurent, "mistress" of Prince Edward. She was seven years his senior and managed his household with competence for twenty-seven years. *Public domain.*

with the appropriate nobility as far as he was concerned. The young prince had dated a couple of other women in Geneva during his adventures and had first met Madame de Saint-Laurent in Geneva as well. She was a widow who happened to be seven years older than the prince.

Prince Edward had smuggled his girlfriend to live with him in Canada to make the best of his difficult banishment. After a long winter in the cold north, the prince and Madame de Saint-Laurent headed south, passing through Burlington with their extensive entourage, gallivanting their way to Boston and New York City. As fun as this may sound, February travel in the great white North was slow and dangerous, to say the least, as the prince would soon find out.

Keep in mind, there were no weather apps, let alone weather forecasts available to hedge one's bets against Mother Nature in the eighteenth century. Traveling on horseback or by sleigh in subfreezing temperatures and drifting snow across frozen landscapes and bodies of water on poorly marked trails was perilous at best. The old New England adage, "If you don't like the weather, just wait a minute, it will change," carried a more foreboding tone back then.

Travel, even with cooperative and healthy horses, could be slow. However, survival chances improved, as almost every other town along the route usually offered a tavern for shelter. But the lodging choices seldom would rate three stars. Rural north country accommodations could vary from a clean, roomy, marginally heated, wood-framed inn to haystacks on the floor of a cold barn. And outdoor privies were still de rigueur.

Nonetheless, the royal entourage sledded down from Montreal on January 22 to Champlain, New York. After staying overnight, they crossed Lake Champlain and sledded south for forty miles to stay at Ebenezer Allen's Two Heroes Inn in the bustling town of South Hero for a night. We should note that South Hero boasted a population of over one thousand residents in 1793, and the Two Heroes Inn was where General Ethan Allen had enjoyed the final party of his life.

The prince's sleighs were impressive but nothing compared to his father's gilded carriage, weighing eight tons and measuring twenty-four feet long and thirteen feet tall. Nonetheless, the teams of crop-eared horses, the military guards in full regalia and the enormous sleighs were extraordinary to behold on the rustic, windswept landscape in northern Vermont. Madame de Saint-Laurent arrived elegantly attired, covered in several fur robes and with a large dog on one of several sleighs. Along with Edward's guest, the entourage included a military escort, bodyguards, attendants and a personal chef. Trunks of food, clothing and other provisions filled up the several sleighs. The prince's valets unloaded more than a dozen carryall trunks of belongings at the Two Heroes Inn.

The next day, the royal entourage reloaded the sleighs and trotted sixteen miles across the ice to Burlington. According to Prince Edward's biographer Mollie Gillen, two of the sleighs carrying the prince's wardrobe crashed through the ice. His entire wardrobe was lost in the lake. According to Gillen, "The Prince had the shock and mortification of seeing two of sleighs, carrying 'the whole of his baggage, consisting of what plate, linen, clothes, &c. He then possessed', fall through the cracking surface into the lake." Prince Edward would replace his haberdashery once he arrived in Boston the following week.

After the near-disaster on the lake, Prince Edward, his girlfriend and the rest of the entourage arrived at the hillside accommodations of Phineas Loomis. They stayed for a couple of nights. Loomis was a fine host and was duly impressed with the prince and his girlfriend. We don't know exactly what the royal chef prepared for the couple, but we can imagine it eclipsed the local Vermont winter diet of smoked meat or fish, canned "sauce" (vegetables) and bread with cider jack or claret wine. We have no more details of Loomis's accommodations, but we do know the prince's bodyguards slept outside his door.

Madame de Saint-Laurent was reportedly more congenial and proper than locals were accustomed to. According to Phineas's son, Horace Loomis, the prince conversed with his girlfriend in French and treated her very kindly. The royal visitors interacted freely with Loomis and other commoners during their stay and later on during their journey south, as we shall see.

Although Madame de Saint-Laurent did not have royal status, by several accounts she was beautiful, clever and witty and managed the prince's household with propriety and competence during their twenty-seven years together. New Hampshire governor Benning Wentworth was a huge fan of hers and was quite smitten. According to Loomis, Prince Edward responded to her very tenderly and kissed her when they departed Burlington.

Upon their departure, Madame de Saint-Laurent headed to New York to visit a friend, and the prince went by a separate route to Boston. According to Loomis, they had plans to rendezvous later on for some fun in the sun in the West Indies.

The prince was good friends with General Henry Knox, a close military advisor and personal friend of General George Washington and socialites in Boston, Philadelphia and New York City. A flurry of social activities erupted when the prince finally cruised into Boston after the fifteen-day journey that had begun on January 22. Several funny stories followed his tour and spread throughout the colonies. A couple of tales bear repeating here, as remembered by biographer Gillen. Note the colloquial humor in context with the times.

In one anecdote, someone asked an outraged man how he felt about his wife being kissed by the prince. The man's retort was, "How does it make the prince feel to get his butt kicked by a tailor?"

Another account sounds like a plausible exchange with some Green Mountain Boy types in Vermont. The story, of the prince and a plain Vermont farmer, tickled funny bones throughout New England.

> *At a tavern, an honest New England man thus accosts him—well how do you do Sir, & are you really the Son of King George?*
> *—he answered that he was, amazing! s'd the man: & how does your daddy do?*
> *—he was well s'd the Prince when I heard last from him*
> *—well now, s'd the honest man, don't you thing* [sic] *he was wrong in Quarrelling with America as he did.*
> *I don't know but he was, s'd the other, but there is no forseeing, at all times, how Matters will turn out.*
> *true, s'd the man, but if it had'nt* [sic] *been for that plaguy Quarrell I suppose he might have been King here yet!*

Victoria, Queen of England and Ireland. *Public domain.*

In the end, the prince and his girlfriend eventually parted ways, and she went to live with her sister. Prince Edward would eventually start acting like a prince and marry Princess Victoria of Saxe-Coburg-Saalfeld. They produced a daughter, who was born in 1819. She was later crowned Victoria, Queen of the United Kingdom, and reigned for sixty-three years.

2

From Illicit to Illustrious

Born out of wedlock in 1760, before the American Revolution, Frances—always known as Fanny—would grow up to be an accomplished multilingual botanist, musician, frontier homemaker and member of Vermont royalty. Twice widowed, she raised ten children, including a couple of West Point graduates and a daughter who became the namesake of an outstanding Vermont hospital. Fanny and her daughter Adelia created the first herbarium in Vermont—possibly the first in the nation. The collection now resides at the Pringle Herbarium at the University of Vermont.

Fanny was born in New York City to a woman named Anna Schoolcraft and a British military officer, General John Montressor. But General Montressor refused to acknowledge Fanny as his daughter, and as a result, she ultimately used the surname Montezuma. Fanny's mother passed away a few years after her birth. Fanny moved in with and was raised by her mother's sister Margaret in New York City. There, Fanny became educated in music, languages and botany. At that time, it was unusual for girls to become educated to such a degree. At best, only a light, superficial education was available for most girls.

Margaret's husband, British colonel Crean Brush, who became Fanny's stepfather, was a Dublin-born attorney and British Tory. An outspoken "Loyalist Yorker," he accumulated twenty thousand acres of land in the New Hampshire Grants, later to become Vermont. He, Margaret and Fanny moved to the Brush estate in Westminster, near the Connecticut River, in 1771.

By 1775, Mr. Brush had become involved in some unscrupulous activity while working for the British in Boston. When the British evacuated the city, Brush was captured, tried for his crimes in an American court and jailed. He spent a year and a half in prison and escaped by dressing up in Margaret's clothes and sneaking past the sentries. Colonel Brush headed back to Westminster to lay low, but his notoriety followed him.

Fanny Montezuma Buchanan Brush Allen Penniman, shown in a portrait completed when she was a young teen. *Public domain.*

About that time, Fanny dated and even became engaged to a British officer. Unfortunately, her fiancé drowned while crossing the Hudson River. At sixteen, Fanny married another British soldier, Captain John Buchanan. Captain Buchanan was killed in 1778 in combat on a privateer mission. Their only child died in 1784. During the time Fanny was coming of age, things were heating up in Vermont territory. But weird coincidences and serendipity seemed to be aligning for Fanny.

COLONEL BRUSH AND COLONEL ALLEN

The Bennington Militia, later known as the Green Mountain Boys, under the leadership of then-Colonel Ethan Allen, had roughed up New York sheriffs as far back as the late 1760s, when the Yorkers had tried to confiscate and tax properties that had been bought by settlers from New Hampshire. In return, Allen and the Green Mountain Boys were making life miserable for the "Loyalist Yorkers" and threatening to confiscate Yorkers' Vermont land and sell it to fund the Vermont militia. One thing is certain: there was no love lost between Colonel Brush, an eloquent Loyalist orator attorney, and Colonel Allen, the vociferous rebel rabble-rouser and land speculator.

Meanwhile, as conflicts between New York officials and settlers in the New Hampshire land grants heated up, Fanny's stepfather, Colonel Brush, posted a bounty on the heads of several of the Green Mountain Boys, including their outspoken leader, Ethan Allen. This is when the story begins to get even more interesting.

In 1775, Ethan Allen co-led, with Benedict Arnold, a daring raid, capturing Fort Ticonderoga and Crown Point. This got the attention of George Washington and King George III. The cannons from those forts were later hauled to Boston and used to force the British fleet of one hundred ships out of Boston Harbor. So, Allen was a big deal. But he was later captured and held in British captivity for almost three years, until 1779.

After finally being released in 1779, Allen began to matriculate back into Vermont society. The hard-living General Ethan Allen, then in his mid-forties, was trying to regain some of his vigor after his malnourished and torturous captivity. He was still grieving the loss of his fourteen-year-old son during his imprisonment, and in 1783, his wife, Mary Brownson Allen, passed away. Not long after that, Fanny Buchanan, then in her mid-twenties, was publicly heard to say she hoped to someday meet the legendary and interesting character named Ethan Allen.

The Stars Align

Fanny soon got her to wish to meet General Allen when he paid her a visit in Westminster. The two found an instant connection, despite their age difference (more than twenty years). From all accounts, there was strong chemistry between them, and they married in Westminster in 1784. Fanny instantly assumed the role of mother of four children by Ethan's first marriage. The couple proceeded to start their own family with the births of Fanny Allen Jr. in 1784, Hannibal Montressor Allen in 1787 and Ethan Voltair Allen, born after Ethan's death, in 1789.

Ethan had his brother Ira build a frame house on 1,500 acres of land near the Onion (Winooski) River in Burlington; Fanny and Ethan moved in during 1787. At that time, there were only a handful of homes within today's boundaries of Burlington. The Allen family—Ethan; Fanny; their children; four kids from Ethan's first marriage; and two servants, Eliza and Newport—all lived in the house. It survives at the Ethan Allen Homestead Museum near the river in Burlington.

The Allens raised livestock and grew crops, and Ethan wrote another book while he lived in Burlington. Fanny raised the children, managed the home and continued her pastime of gardening with herbal, medicinal, edible and other practical plants. Flax was spun into linen thread and milled into cloth, and other plants were used to make dyes.

In 1789, Ethan Allen suffered a stroke and passed away, leaving Fanny pregnant and with a full house of children and no legal will. The coverture laws of the time left surviving widows only the linens and not much else of the estate. To make it worse, no legal documents existed to prove that Ethan had actually owned a title to the house and acreage he had earlier negotiated in a gentleman's agreement with his cash-strapped brother Ira. But Fanny's stepfather, Colonel Brush, had passed away and left her one-third of his remaining estate in Westminster.

FANNY'S NEW FAMILY

The ever-resilient Fanny and the kids moved back to Westminster to live. She met twice-widowed Dr. Jabez Penniman. They married in 1793. Penniman repeatedly appealed to Ira Allen to pay for school for Ethan's children and to relinquish his claim to Ethan's estate. Jabez and Fanny Penniman sued Ira. After several years in court, the Pennimans prevailed.

The Pennimans moved into the old Ethan Allen homestead in Burlington, where they lived for a few years and eventually built a farm on a bluff in Colchester and lived there happily for thirty more years. This property was located at the corner of Route 15 and Lime Kiln Road, across the road from today's St. Michael's College. The farm property is thought to be the source of Fanny and Adelia's herbarium. Dr. Penniman served as a town clerk, Vermont Assembly representative, probate judge and a University of Vermont trustee. Fanny delivered and raised four Penniman children in Burlington and Colchester.

In 1814, Fanny and her youngest daughter, Adelia, began to assemble a sizable catalog of pressed native plants. The plants were painstakingly mounted on eight-by-thirteen-inch paper and inscribed with common names, scientific names and symbolic plant names. Two French botanists had visited Burlington a decade earlier, and it is plausible that Fanny interacted with them. One of those visitors, French botanist André Michaux, had recently published the first book on plant nomenclature, so this may be why Fanny was at the forefront of botany and nomenclature.

Eventually, the herbarium of two hundred plants was left to the Pringle Herbarium at the University of Vermont, where it resides today. The earthly

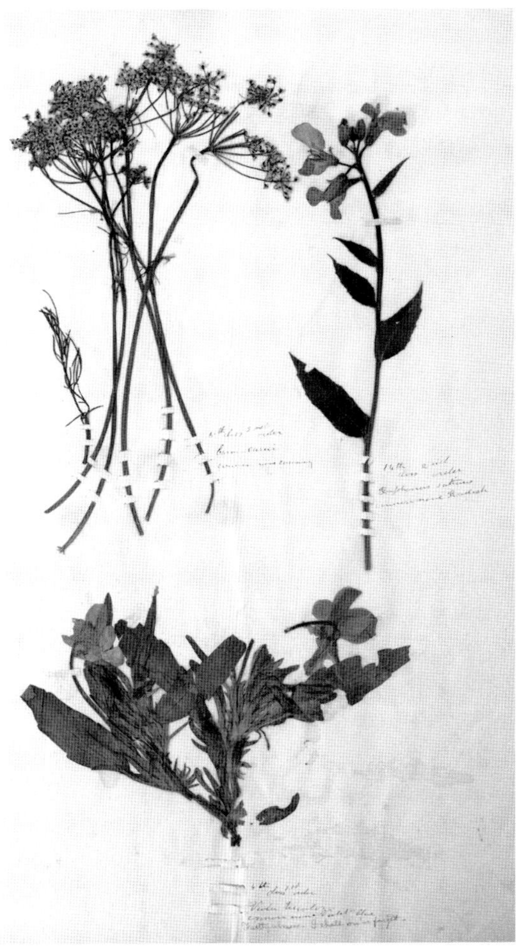

Caraway, radish, blue violet, "Faithfulness. I shall ne'er forget," from Fanny and Adelia's herbarium. *Pringle Herbarium, UVM.*

remains of Adelia, Jabez and Fanny lie side by side in Elmwood Cemetery in Burlington, where many other Burlington celebrities were interred. Fanny's horizontal headstone reads: "Frances Montezuma Penniman / Wife of Jabez Penniman / Formerly wife of Gen. Ethan Allen."

Ethan and Fanny's two boys graduated from West Point. Fanny Junior graduated from a convent in Montreal and followed her path to becoming a nun. She was Vermont's first Catholic nun and nurse. She returned to Burlington to treat sick soldiers during the War of 1812 at the Battery Park military base hospital. In the late 1800s, the Fanny Allen Hospital Hotel Dieu was founded in her honor by the Edmundites of Montreal on the acreage that was formerly Jabez Penniman's farm. Today, the Fanny Allen Campus is part of the University of Vermont Health Care Network.

3

A Crazy Twist

Even though the only state mental hospital was named the "Vermont Asylum for the Insane," the institution was still ahead of its time, employing humane treatment practices in the 1860s. The asylum boasted beautiful grounds, healthy activities, community-integrated programs, locavore food and least-restrictive confinement practices. But a series of embarrassing court cases embroiled the asylum in two comprehensive state investigations during the 1870s. The story leading up to the investigation might be worthy of a screenplay. At the very least, two patients, J.S. and P.S., who met for the first time at the asylum, became good friends and collaborated to challenge the integrity of and practices at the institution.

In 1869, J.S. was committed to the Brattleboro asylum after having been judged a "lunatic" in Pennsylvania. He had resided in three different asylums for about two years each in that state and had been placed under guardianship before being committed to Brattleboro. J.S. claimed to have previously been a war veteran and had attained the rank of colonel. He looked smart, presented himself with some pretense, seemed to be well read and was a published author.

We have all known people whose personal net worth and accomplishments seem to increase exponentially with the distance they are from home. J.S. evidently took this expertise to a whole new level.

His diagnosed mental illness was monomania, a nineteenth-century psychiatric diagnosis for someone limited in expression to only one idea or area of thought. During the dawn of psychiatry, monomania was seen as a dangerous madness. But this diagnosis would soon suffer a backlash in the realm of public opinion, and this story marks that turning point and clarifies the slippery slope of defining monomania and moral insanity.

According to the annals of the asylum, J.S. engaged in long, pervasive habits of intemperance, with a disposition to exaggerate and misrepresent and to possess irrepressible conceit and a passion for heroic notoriety. When presented with facts proving his insanity, J.S. showed an ever-fluent and plausible ability to argue speciously, and he was disruptive and rebellious everywhere he went. He was always getting into trouble and promoting disaffection in the institution, and he became the oracle of others with disordered minds and derangement. He boldly charged that many in the asylum were not insane and convincingly accused the asylum officers of mercenary motives. He preferred to act behind the scenes with demoralizing rhetoric and activities. In short, he was a manipulative troublemaker.

At the Brattleboro Asylum, J.S. made the acquaintance of another monomaniac, a seventy-one-year-old Presbyterian clergyman, P.S., who suffered from "dyspepsia"—known today as indigestion—among other ailments. After his physician advised him to eat less meat, he became a vegetarian and went on a crusade for that cause and to promote his new lifestyle. This might be considered normal today. However, P.S. became so overly obsessed in his behavior that his mental health suffered severely.

Early in his career, P.S. started a family and found a congregation, only to lose it when he had a breakdown after being left out of his family will. He found a second congregation, but that lasted only a few years. He became even more distraught when his son decided he did not want to follow in his footsteps as a minister. By age forty, P.S. had become indigent and unable to provide for his family. He succumbed to "morbid inertia," stayed in his room and forbade family in his house except for his kids. Then his wife died. Eventually, he found himself in Barnet, Vermont, living like a pauper, in his seventies and infirm. At the request of the Barnet Selectboard and the Overseer of the Poor, P.S. was committed to the Brattleboro Asylum and found to be insane by the doctors there. An asylum doctor described P.S. as egotistical, overbearing, without a purpose, strongly prejudiced and unable to change his mind once he made it up.

J.S. and P.S. became best friends and formed a mutual admiration society in the asylum. They seemed to feed off each other, with J.S. playing the part of the mastermind and P.S. the unflagging cheerleader and advocate. On May 30, 1872, J.S. "eloped" from the Brattleboro Asylum by climbing over the wall and walking fifty miles to Windsor. He resurfaced one hundred miles away in the queen city of Burlington, Vermont.

Once in Burlington, J.S. made fast friends with anyone who would listen to his authoritative and captivating soliloquies, and his audience grew as he built a compelling case against his unlawful commitment at the Brattleboro Asylum. One can imagine the Burlington boomtown at the peak of the textile and shipping economy, with a lively social setting in the watering holes and businesses. Distilleries, breweries and taverns overflowed with products and customers. Bundles of money moved from the shipping companies and mills into the bank vaults, and stylish mansions were sprouting up on the hill. It must have been quite a social scene with a ready audience hungry for entertainment.

The men in the white coats soon tracked down J.S. in Burlington. But before he could be returned to Brattleboro, his attorney, R.H. Start, brought him before Chief Justice John Pierpoint with an act of habeas corpus at the Vermont Supreme Court, which happened to be in Burlington. At that time, the supreme court was mobile and sat in each county throughout the year. The court was not a panel, as it is today. Rather, a single judge had jurisdiction over all general litigation. Justice Pierpoint, learning that J.S. was under guardianship because of insanity, recommitted him to the asylum. But not so fast. J.S. had attracted the best legal minds in Burlington to represent him. After a hearing in the Windham County Chancery Court, the second writ of habeas corpus resulted in J.S. going before another judge in U.S. Court.

Attorney R.H. Start filed the second writ on the grounds that the prior judge had no jurisdiction in the case, since J.S. was technically a resident of another state. The U.S. Court judge set the hearing date for a couple of months later, on August 2, for a full investigation into its merits. J.S. was remanded to the charge of the proper officer with directions "to restrain him no more than might be necessary to have him present at such hearing." J.S. had no intentions of going anywhere. Things were just getting good for him. He enjoyed all of the amenities that Burlington had to offer for the two beautiful months of June and July, and his legal counsel got right to work.

According to the *Annals of the Vermont Asylum for the Insane*, on July 2, J.S. sent a letter from Burlington to an attendant at the Brattleboro Asylum with the following message:

> *My friends are going to make it a very interesting trial. I secured three good attorneys here, two more have volunteered, and there will be others. Gov. Stewart will be invited to be present, so he can understand the workings of and at the*

1871 Burlington Courthouse on Church Street. *Library of Congress.*

> *Asylum. Of course,* [Dr.] *Lovejoy will be here, so Dr. Tenney and I will have a good week's work. I have to thank him for being made a lion of. I have quite distinguished visitors hourly, but, think of it, bouquets of flowers almost equal to those on J——— F———'s grave!*

We can only imagine Superintendent Dr. William Rockwell's reaction to this turn of events and the letter from J.S. Rockwell had recently resigned due to a disastrous fall from his carriage. His assistant, Joseph Draper, had taken over as superintendent. Nonetheless, Rockwell died the following year. Immediately before the next court hearing, a letter from relatives of J.S. was published in the *Burlington Free Press* that said J.S. was not a colonel and, in fact, had never served his country. They went on to claim that he was a complete imposter. But it wouldn't make much of a difference.

J.S. had found ready sympathizers and sharp attorneys in Burlington lining up to not only represent his case but also exert pressure for an investigation of the Brattleboro Asylum for the Insane by the Vermont legislature, which was to convene in October. At the hearing in August, both sides presented their testimonies.

J.S. was judged sane by Judge David Allen Smalley in the U.S. District Court hearing and unconditionally discharged. Following the judgment for J.S. and pending the October investigation of the Brattleboro asylum. J.S. alerted his legal counsel and fanned the flames for them to represent his buddy P.S., who was still living at the asylum.

Legal proceedings began with a writ of habeas corpus for P.S. He, too, was brought before Judge Smalley at the Burlington Courthouse and discharged as sane on September 5. During the hearing, the seventy-eight-year-old P.S. took the stand and made a strong case for his sanity. The judge ruled that the burden of proof was on the asylum to show that P.S. was not a resident of New York in the first place. The asylum superintendent testified that he had no interest in P.S.'s residency. Judge Smalley ascertained that P.S. showed no signs of being insane during the hearing and released him from state custody.

The ensuing state investigation put the Brattleboro Asylum through the wringer and dug far deeper than the illegal commitment question. It focused on ownership and control, alleged crowded conditions, abusive treatment and wrongful confinement. The state inquiry was followed by one in 1876. In it, independent commissioners were brought by another disgruntled former patient, who at the time worked for the state as the commissioner of the insane. It dragged on for years.

Even though the investigations exonerated the asylum and concluded that it had followed sound practices and leadership, the cases pointed to the desperate need for another asylum for the long-term chronically ill. This would allow Brattleboro to get back to what it did so well, which was working with those who were curable and concentrating on humane treatment. These cases also challenged the definition of insanity and highlighted questions about confinement, which would become big issues in the coming decades. The labels used in mental health have changed significantly in 150 years. If nothing else, this story points out how much the definition of insanity has changed.

After their release from the Brattleboro Asylum in 1872, both men returned to their home states. J.S. was pronounced insane once again and returned to a private institution in Pennsylvania; he died there shortly thereafter. P.S. returned to Brooklyn and lived in the care of his adult daughter for a while, then in the care of his son. He died in a New York boarding hotel within a couple of years.

4
The Father of Modern Education

Burlington's first public high school, originally an "academy for advanced scholars" and eventually known as Burlington Academy, was established in 1816. By the turn of the nineteenth century, thirty-five school principals had come and gone, which might rival modern school administrator tenures. But 1859 was a big year in the town. The newly named Burlington High School (BHS) eliminated tuition, finally admitted females for the first time and committed to a forty-six-week school year. But that's not all that happened in that eventful year.

In 1859, a rock star was born in Burlington. John Dewey evolved into one of the world's foremost social philosophers and promoters of active learning in the nineteenth and twentieth centuries. His imprint on teaching and learning thrives today.

According to his biographer George Dykhuizen, the Dewey family lived at 14 George Street in Burlington from 1867 to 1876, across the street from Civil War hero General George Stannard's brick house, which still stands on the west corner of Pearl and George Streets. (The Dewey house, on the east side of George Street, was demolished in 1957 to make space for the parking lot of the then-new Federal Building on Pearl Street.) The Deweys moved to 178 Pearl Street in the spring of 1876, and John attended the Murray Street School (now the site of Lawrence Barnes School), which had been built in 1857. By the time Dewey was a teen, BHS had relocated to the northwest corner of South Willard and College Streets. His father, Archibald S. Dewey, owned a grocery store at 119 St. Paul Street. One of the greatest American minds originated from the heart of Burlington.

John Dewey, Burlington native, philosopher and innovative educator. *Library of Congress.*

We don't know for sure if Dewey's schooling at BHS, attending services and Sunday school at the First Congregational Church, earning a BA at UVM or teaching high school during winter term in Charlotte, Vermont, inspired his views on learning and life. But we do know that he was and still is a legend with those who take teaching and learning seriously. He was anything but old school. Among other accomplishments, Dewey cofounded the NAACP and the precursor organization to the American Civil Liberties Union but later withdrew when that organization appeared to become infiltrated with Communists. During his productive life, Dewey found time to author over forty books. But that wasn't all there was to write home about.

Compliments for Dewey and his influence flowed from the ivory towers and highest offices in America. President Harry Truman called Dewey "one of the greatest Americans." Lyndon Baines Johnson was inspired by Dewey to not lose faith in one's fellow man and found the name for his domestic program, the Great Society, in Dewey's writing. Historian Henry Steele Commager said that for a generation "no major issue was clarified until Dewey had spoken." UVM president Matthew Buckham, who had graduated as valedictorian from UVM at age nineteen, said Dewey had a "logical, thorough-going, absolutely independent mind; sound and sweet all through." On Dewey's ninetieth birthday, Columbia professor Irwin Edman described him as a "homespun, almost regional, character… one would imagine oneself talking with a Vermont countryman." This is remarkable considering the heights Dewey attained.

After penning two journal articles titled "The Metaphysical Assumptions of Materialism" and "The Pantheism of Spinoza," he was accepted by the Johns Hopkins philosophy PhD program and, upon graduation, published *Psychology*, a book that earned him the nickname "parent of behavioral psychology." Dewey spent a decade at the University of Michigan and then was snapped up by the University of Chicago, where, in 1896, with his wife, Alice Chipman, he established the Laboratory School. The lab consisted of sixteen pupils and two teachers, an ideal teacher-to-student ratio. Active learning prevailed in that setting.

Instead of learning within rigid subjects and fixed student-teacher roles, Dewey believed that learning should be about making connections and making decisions based on context. He encouraged students to think laterally, critically and creatively; to reveal connections; and to form their own original insights. Today, this kind of education is associated with high quality student-centered learning, theme-based learning and problem-based learning.

As an example of this method, when learning about trade routes and geopolitics, in one activity, students sat at their desks with bits of raw cotton and wool and were asked to make fibers out of them that could be woven. Dewey asked questions such as "Why is it that we wear more wool than cotton?" Students noted that seeds needed to be removed from the cotton. Then Dewey asked where the cotton was grown and who picked it. This would open a discussion about slavery in the American South. A further question asked where else cotton was grown. The answer was, in places like Egypt. This would continue with a discussion on trade routes and geopolitics.

What big ideas did Dewey promote that changed philosophy, psychology and education? When intelligence testing was all the rage, he dissented, believing that all students have an inborn curiosity that should be nurtured. He believed that nurturing, not necessarily social status or inherent wealth, led to better ideas and decision-making.

Dewey believed that humans come to their fullest potential in the context of working with others. Social interactions offer the opportunity for democracy to evolve, and we cannot separate ourselves from our social context and membership in the community. He believed in a fundamental principle of schools as a form of community life. Rather than promote the existing social order, he believed that schools needed to improve the economic, legal and political order.

He understood that life presented ever-changing problems and that preparing students for only one set of problems by drilling them with facts when new facts continually arise wasn't enough. Instead, he sought to increase students' ability to respond to new situations intelligently. He believed this would come when students learned to suspend judgment, show skepticism, desire evidence, observation, discussion and inquiry. They should not make biased decisions or necessarily follow convention.

After his stint at the University of Chicago, "Dr. Johnny," as he was known, worked at Columbia University for half a century. In 1929, he became president of the League for Independent Political Action, which intended to become a party. He cited that both Democrats and

Republicans had become errand boys for big business and not for the working people.

John Dewey died in 1952. His ashes are buried next to Ira Allen Chapel overlooking the UVM green in Burlington.

Dewey's ideas were big during his life, and they are timely today, when talking about race and class can be uncomfortable and contentious. Following Dewey's ideas, we see students taking action to address injustices of the past and to avoid them in the present and future.

For example, students at BHS and other schools have protested for equal pay in professional soccer. Students have participated in women's marches and the climate strike and flown the Black Lives Matter flag on campus. Gun-safety walkouts took place after the Parkland massacre. Students have also participated in successful lobbying of the legislature for their right to free speech.

Today's students are engaged in democracy, research, deep thinking, logic, active learning and political action to improve their world. And lest we forget, many of them are voters. Burlington's rock star, the father of modern education, would be proud.

5
The Admiral of Lake Champlain

A 1790 diary describes Burlington as having only three buildings in the village near the waterfront. All three were lakefront properties on Water Street, now known as Battery Street. One building, Gideon King Sr.'s tavern, a two-story structure with a kitchen in the rear that stood at the northeast corner of King and Water Streets, served as the courthouse at that time. The other two buildings were Job Boynton's broad, wood-frame house and John Collins's 1778 home. Boynton had arrived in 1780; King came with his family in 1788.

At that time, one of King's four sons, Gideon King Jr., was a teenager and was already involved in the shipping business in Burlington Bay. He was the King who would make the biggest splash in the lucrative industry. Lake Champlain was the main transportation route, whether by paddle, sail or sleigh over ice in the winter. This was because paths over land were scant and roads nonexistent.

Before long, Gid King Jr. had built dozens of ships with names such as *Dolphin*, *Privateer*, *Essex*, *Maria*, *Richard* and *Boxer*. For three decades, King controlled virtually all of the shipping between St. John, Quebec, to the north and Whitehall, New York, to the south. He owned all of the wharves in Burlington, so other ship captains were forced to lease space from him or would have to find their own way to shore.

By 1798, Gid Jr. had bought Job Boynton's new brick house on a lot with outbuildings and an orchard at 35 King Street. There is controversy and speculation about whether the "Gideon King House" at 35 King dates to 1790 or whether it was reconstructed in 1798, or even as late as 1830. Regardless of the date, that building represents Burlington's first economic boom on the waterfront.

The Gideon King House at 35 King Street. *Courtesy of the author.*

King's fortunes rose as he became the largest shipbuilder in the Champlain Valley and held mortgages on virtually all Lake Champlain shipping fleets in Burlington and Whitehall, New York. Burlington Bay was initially shallow, with the shoreline extending to the base of Water Street. Big ships couldn't get to shore with their deeper drafts. Historian William S. Rann describes captains tossing beef, pork and liquor barrels into the bay and letting them drift to shore. Dry goods were put on "lighters"—shallow-bottom boats—and rowed to shore. Over time, much of the bay near the shore was filled in and wharves extended into the lake as a part of the shipping infrastructure.

In the early 1800s, King's all-or-nothing shipping empire put him squarely at odds with the political challenges of the time. It would be choppy sailing for a while. A British frigate fired on an American ship, killing three Americans and injuring eighteen. Sailors from the frigate then boarded and removed four alleged former British citizens to serve under the British flag. President Thomas Jefferson then took action. He wrote the Embargo Act of 1807 to punish France and Britain for interfering in American trade while they were at war with each other. Jefferson hoped that restricting American trade would force Britain and France to recognize American neutrality.

The U.S. Congress added a land embargo by the spring of 1808; that is when tempers became a tempest. The embargo threatened to hobble the Vermont economy. For most northern Vermonters, economic survival depended on shipping north to larger population centers in Canada. As a result, smuggling over the land and lake ramped up and continued, regardless of the law.

Vermont's Jabez Penniman, the man who had married Ethan Allen's widow, Fanny, a few years earlier, was appointed to the unenviable position of collector of customs by President Jefferson in 1803. Penniman complained that the new embargo law, which eliminated legal shipping to Canada, would not be enforceable without adequate government power. Jefferson responded in no uncertain terms that anyone breaking the law by smuggling across the border would be apprehended by any means possible, including force and arms.

Burlington (and most of the towns in the Champlain Valley) held town meetings in April to discuss the "ruinous" new law and how to avert it. The anti-embargo fervor erupted like a chain reaction all across the state. Penniman hired militiamen in an attempt to enforce the embargo on the lake. But as Vermonters know, "everyone knows everyone in Vermont." It was even more the case then. Often, the militiamen knew the merchants and shippers, let alone the reality that many families were dependent on revenue from commerce with Canada for their survival.

After the militia failed to enforce the law, new enforcers were hired, skirmishes ensued and rumors about violent clashes multiplied. Penniman tried to reassure the public and drown out the rumors, claiming there hadn't been any killings, injuries or boat runaways. Penniman even quipped that (Gid) King had not killed him yet.

Later on, Penniman admitted that smuggling of all kinds of produce was rampant over land and on the lake. Experienced merchants such as Gideon King knew all too well that the sprawling Missisquoi Bay straddling the border included many miles of U.S. and Canadian land frontage. Since British and American ships continuously ferried products on the bay to their own respective ports, it became next to impossible to control twenty-four-hour smuggling going from the United States to Canada on the bay. In addition, regardless of where they were on the lake, boats often used the cover of darkness and a strong south wind to their advantage at the border. After anchoring until nightfall, the armed crew would weigh the anchor and sail over the border. The enforcers didn't have the manpower to stop them from making a run into Canada.

The embargo stoked conflict and polarization, and things were getting testy, to say the least. On August 3, 1808, an incident occurred on the Winooski River between the present location of the Gardeners Supply Store and the Ethan Allen Homestead. This would lead to Vermont's first murder trial and a public hanging in front of thousands of spectators in Burlington. Here's how it played out.

Before the embargo, a boat named the *Black Snake* had been a single-masted ferry for passengers between Charlotte, Vermont, and Essex, New York. On August 3, it was in service smuggling barrels of potash, which was in high demand. Potash was wood ash lye used in a variety of products, including soaps, dyes, glass, baked goods and gunpowder.

The *Black Snake* wasn't pretty. It had been painted black with tar, hence its name. It was powered by the sail and seven oars and protected by a "wall gun," which was a mounted, seventy-five-pound, large-diameter flintlock shotgun. The fact that the crew would be armed with a mounted gun tells us all we need to know about the nature of bootlegging at the time.

As the federalized militia boarded and attempted to confiscate the *Black Snake* and its illegal cargo of potash, the smugglers opened fire on the militia. Several people were killed, including officers and an innocent bystander. A trial was held in Burlington. Vermont Supreme Court judge Royall Tyler presided over a jury that included Ethan Allen Jr., who happened to be an unabashed smuggling advocate. An interesting side note is that pro and con commentaries were published by Allen Jr. and Jabez Penniman—Allen's stepfather—in the same April 15, 1808 *Sentinel and Democrat* newspaper. The nineteen-year-old Allen railed on the "anti-Republican" "fag end of the embargo," while Penniman reiterated that armed boats would apprehend smugglers by force if necessary. Their conflict must have made for some interesting family dinnertime conversations.

Of the several *Black Snake* smugglers who were accused, a man named Cyrus Dean was convicted of murder and sentenced to be hanged to death. The other defendants, who perhaps enjoyed better legal maneuvering, drew lighter sentences, including time in the stockades, whipping and prison time.

According to historian William S. Rann, Daniel Staniford was the sheriff and executioner. A gallows was constructed especially for Cyrus Dean on a little knoll just east of what is now the site of Mary Fletcher's house on today's North Prospect Street. There were no roads nearby at the time, and the landscape was covered by second-growth pine.

On November 11, 1808, the procession marched from the jail on Church Street up the Pearl Street hill and cut through a lane by Henry Loomis's house. There, in the woods, thousands watched as Dean was hanged on the gallows. It was the first and only execution recorded in Burlington.

In the end, both Embargo Acts were abysmal failures. Smugglers adapted so well to the law that exports from Vermont increased as much as 30 percent during the first year. There were accounts of so many livestock walking up the eastern shoreline of Lake Champlain that they packed down a solid road into Canada!

Eventually, the embargo was lifted and trading with Canada became legal again. As the War of 1812 heated up, Gid King capitalized on government contracts to transport American troops and supplies throughout the Champlain Valley. Finally, in 1821, King transferred his business assets, including ships and wharves, to the Lake Champlain Steamboat Company in return for a small fortune in shares of that company. The admiral of the lake died in 1829 as a new era of growth was emerging.

6

Burlington's Greatest Philanthropist

Today, Vermont's largest employer, the UVM Medical Center, owes its existence to a shy, infirm woman who was committed to bestowing the gift of health on the people of Burlington. The story begins in 1828, when Thaddeus Fletcher married Mary Laurence Peaslee of Gilmantown, New Hampshire. They moved to Vermont, built a modest homestead in Essex Center and, before long, produced five children. Only two of the children survived to adulthood. The second-born child, Mary Martha, watched most of her siblings die as children. Even though public school wasn't available for girls at that time, while still living in Essex, Mary and the surviving sibling, Ellen, attended the Burlington Female Seminary, which was located at the site of today's Converse Home on lower Church Street. The school, which had been established around 1836, offered a rich liberal arts education in music, drawing, painting, Italian and German. Both girls were remembered as being in delicate health.

Thaddeus Fletcher's mercantile business enterprise thrived, and by the mid-1800s, he was said to have amassed an extraordinary net worth of half a million dollars. By 1850, Fletcher transitioned into semi-retirement and built a brick house on North Prospect Street in Burlington and moved his family there.

Fletcher's two daughters continued to go to school in Burlington. Both were sick throughout their lives. Ellen died of consumption, now known as tuberculosis (TB), in 1857, when Mary was twenty-seven years old. Mary

Mary Martha Fletcher. *Public domain.*

continued to live with her parents. She also struggled with her physical health and was a victim of long-term TB. The family was supported by their hired handyman, Henry Murphy, and Anna O'Connor, an Irish American housekeeper.

Thaddeus Fletcher was a generous man. While still alive, he made donations to fund educational institutions in Burlington. He hoped that part of his fortune would go to start a hospital to treat people for various diseases. Smallpox, typhus, dysentery, TB and other diseases were still common. But hospitals for the general public were unusual at a time when doctors made house calls, and remedies were often remarkably different from those today. The Fletchers believed a hospital would be an asset to the community and would conceivably treat all kinds of illnesses as the population of Burlington grew.

Thaddeus Fletcher passed away in 1871. His fortune was left to his trusted wife, Mary L. Fletcher. Mrs. Fletcher, daughter Mary and the staff continued to live in the house on Prospect Street. In 1873, Mrs. Fletcher made a $10,000 gift for books to the city of Burlington, and her daughter Mary matched it with a $10,000 gift to erect a library building. It would be known as the Fletcher Free Library. It stands today as an architectural landmark and part of the heart and soul of the city. Mrs. Fletcher passed away unexpectedly from a stroke in 1876, leaving her daughter alone.

Mary wanted to respect her parents' wishes and build a hospital in Burlington, which would be the first nonmilitary hospital in the state of Vermont. But she wouldn't be able to do it herself. Paul Buckham, the president of UVM, helped Mary procure land at the thirty-five-acre Moses Catlin farm on the top of the hill in Burlington, next to the UVM campus. Mary purchased the Catlin farm for $25,000. It included a farmhouse, a coach barn, outbuildings, orchards, gardens, groves and pastures. The legislature quickly passed an act of incorporation for a nonprofit hospital in Burlington, and Governor Fairbanks signed it into law.

As Mary's health deteriorated as a result of TB, she made final preparations for the project with President Buckham and donated over $100,000 to create the hospital. The farm buildings were moved off the land or torn down. Vermont-born Boston architect W.P. Wentworth completed the design. Construction began in 1877. All of the materials for the building and

Mary Fletcher Hospital original building. *Courtesy of the author.*

furniture were locally procured, and the hospital opened its doors to the first patient in 1879. Mary lived another six years and was able to help establish a four-week-long nursing degree program. The nursing school welcomed its first class in 1882, and she participated in some of the activities in the first few years of the program.

Mary's final wish was to die in the new twenty-nine-bed Mary Fletcher Hospital. When Mary's physician made his last house call to her home on Prospect Street in 1885, he knew she was gravely ill. She pleaded with him to take her to the hospital for the end of her life. The doctor complied with her wish and loaded her on his carriage to take the last ride down Prospect Street, up Pearl Street and up the winding driveway to the new hospital on the hill. Mary Fletcher passed away in the hospital on her own terms shortly thereafter.

Mary left an additional $200,000 to the hospital, at the time the largest sum ever given away in Vermont. Her final act was to donate a "free bed" at the hospital in the form of $5,000 in the name of the First Calvinistic Congregational Church of Burlington. Other philanthropists soon followed Mary's example by endowing free beds to patients at the hospital.

Over the past century, the hospital has evolved through several name changes and transformative construction projects and has continued to be the largest and most sophisticated hospital in Vermont. The Mary Fletcher Hospital is currently named the University of Vermont Medical Center. It looks very different than it did in 1879, when it accepted its first patient.

II

ORIGIN STORIES

7

Welcome to Deerfield!

As many Vermont history lovers know, the first colonial settlers encountered a pristine wilderness in a state of constant uncertainty and turmoil. And Vermont wasn't even a state yet. In fact, during the 1760s and through the 1780s, Vermont territory was still in a three-way tug-of-war among New York to the west, New Hampshire to the east and, on occasion, the Massachusetts Bay Colony to the south. In 1763, long before any European settlers arrived in 1772 to set up shop, the New Hampshire governor, Benning Wentworth, chartered the town of Burlington. In 1766, the same acreage was chartered by the governor of New York as Deerfield, New York. Wait. What? Really?

To understand the conflicting charters, we need to know a bit about what was going on around Burlington—err, Deerfield. The first twinkle in Vermont's eye shone in the year 1749, when New Hampshire governor Benning Wentworth, a wealthy British merchant from Portsmouth, chartered Bennington. "Benning town" would be the first town established in the area between Lake Champlain and the Connecticut River by New Hampshire. Keep in mind that Westminster (now Vermont) had already been chartered by the Massachusetts Bay Colony in 1735. In fact, the Massachusetts Bay Colony claimed the entire present-day state of Maine as well. As time went on, Governor Wentworth continued chartering towns in the same neck of the woods as his namesake town. Wentworth had plenty of incentive, since he allocated five hundred prime acres in each town for himself. He was also savvy enough to name a lot of the towns after wealthy English lords, knowing this would fuel support with the nobility back in his mother country. Several Burlington names exist in England, so there is a plausible explanation for the origin of the town name.

Top: Benning Wentworth, New Hampshire governor from 1741 to 1766. *Public domain.*

Bottom: George Clinton, New York governor (1777–95, 1801–4), later served as vice president (1805–12). *Public domain.*

Unfortunately, Wentworth's town charters in the Champlain Valley and the western Connecticut River Valley wilderness did not go over well with the governors in New York. They insisted that New York owned the territory that extended eastward, over to the Connecticut River.

By 1760, New York governor Cadwallader Colden strenuously objected to Governor Wentworth's selling of land grants and sent him letters to that effect. But the long-reigning Wentworth coldly ignored Colden and subsequent New York governors. New York officially protested Wentworth's moves to King George III. After deliberation, the king's Privy Council in 1764 ruled in favor of New York. Colden and subsequent New York governors, including William Tryon and George Clinton, proclaimed the land between Lake Champlain and the Connecticut River as their territory. After a brief respite from selling more land grants, Wentworth continued to deal New Hampshire town grants on a regular basis. Because the land grants were relatively inexpensive, there was no shortage of buyers. And they came for a variety of reasons.

The Great Awakening religious fervor that was spreading in Massachusetts and Connecticut alienated some of the residents, prompting some settlers to seek a place with freer attitudes than those with Puritanical religious practices. Some wanted a fresh start in the land of milk and honey, and others chased riches in land speculation. As a result, thousands of settlers from the crowded colony of Connecticut and farms of western Massachusetts streamed northward

Ira Allen, one of the early grant holders of a majority of Burlington's acreage. *Public domain.*

to wilderness forests, rivers, lakes and greener pastures in what would become Vermont.

The settlers found tens of thousands of acres selling at bargain-basement prices, thanks to Wentworth. The land was full of timber and potential water power in the flowing rivers and held the potential of success. What hardworking European settler could turn down an opportunity to start a better life, raise a big family and run a farm or other business in a new frontier that had yet to be established? And if the arduous farm and timber life didn't offer enough opportunity, there was also the possibility of getting in on the ground floor of real estate using its first rule: "Location, location, location." Buyers had the chance to flip improved acreage for more than they paid for it. In this way, they hoped to adhere to the second rule of real estate: "Buy low, sell high." Land speculation became a goal for a good number of men.

After being snubbed by Wentworth, a succession of New York governors sent sheriffs with large security detachments into the territory to evict settlers who had bought New Hampshire grants. The sheriffs attempted to sell the settlers New York land patents for the land they had already purchased from New Hampshire. Some of the settlers had built cabins and farms and prospered on their homesteads. Not only were sheriffs evicting settlers, but New York also sent tax collectors to collect money from New Hampshire grantees. Even if the grantees wanted to buy New York patents or pay taxes, currency was scarce.

During the 1760s, the persistent "Yorkers," as they were called in the Bennington area, were met with hostility. An ad hoc Bennington militia was formed to deny them success, intimidate them and send them packing back to Albany. Ethan Allen became the charismatic and vociferous leader of the militia, which later was called the Green Mountain Boys. It is worth noting that this group included brothers Ira Allen, Zimri Allen and Heman Allen and their cousin Remember Baker, among three hundred other ruffians. Remember those names, as they would form the Onion River Land Company, which owned nearly 70 percent of Burlington by the 1770s.

New York persisted in trying to sell its own land patents in the future Vermont territory, although it had a hard time with it. Eventually, the Green Mountain Boys earned a reputation with the New York authorities. And the New York deeds were not equal to the New Hampshire deeds. At first glance, the New Hampshire land grant deeds and the New York land patents appeared similar, but the details were markedly different.

Here are the first few lines of the Burlington charter from New Hampshire:

> *Burlington*
> *GEORGE THE THIRD,*
> *By the Grace of GOD, of Great-Britain, France and Ireland, KING, Defender of the Faith &c.*
> *To all Persons to who these Presents shall come, Greeting, for the province of New Hampshire.*

Here are the first few lines of the Deerfield charter from New York:

> *Deerfield*
> *GEORGE the Third by the Grace of God of Great Britain, France and Ireland, King Defender of the Fait and so forth. To all whom these Presents shall come Greeting, from the province of New York.*

We will spare the reader the task of perusing pejorative references to the "humble subjects" and the patronizing genuflection toward the "well-beloved governor," let alone the convoluted and sometimes indecipherable descriptions of the boundaries in each case. But suffice it to say that both charters seem to describe approximately the same thirty-five thousand acres, more or less, bordering Lake Champlain and the Winooski River on two sides, and including some or all of present-day Williston, South Burlington and Richmond.

Overall, the New Hampshire deed reads more clearly than the New York version and is somewhat more understandable to a layperson today. It spells out the town boundaries on four sides with less ambiguity. It even proclaims that there will be an annual meeting to elect officers and conduct business. This set the stage for annual Vermont town meetings that persist today. But the New Hampshire grants also offered quality-of-life assets that the New York patents did not. The New Hampshire grants allocated land for a parish for "The Church of England" and schools in their town charters.

By contrast, the 1766 New York deed measures the dimensions of the town in "chains," a measurement that didn't withstand the test of time. If that wasn't enough, the patent used carved notches on trees as survey markers. It also makes no provision for churches and schools in each town.

Reading deeper into the two deeds, the New York system paralleled the English manor system; the acreage in the New York patents was generally larger, and the large-acreage land patents could be afforded only by the wealthy and well connected. The wealthy New York manor lord patent owners would then lease their land to small farmers, who could enjoy the privilege of building their homes or business operations without owning or building equity in their land. This suited the Loyalist-leaning New York establishment quite well. New York was already a well-established gigantic landmass with lots of natural resources.

In the end, Ira Allen and his musket-toting crew of ruffians chased Yorker surveyors off Burlington-area land in the early 1770s under the threat of death. The Yorkers never returned. The 1763 New Hampshire charter for the town of Burlington stuck, and the 1766 patent for Deerfield became hidden in history. New York was miffed enough to keep Vermont out of the union until 1791.

The first Burlington proprietors' meeting was held in Salisbury, Connecticut, on March 14, 1774. A proprietor's meeting was a precursor to a town meeting before there was a town. The attendees of that meeting included the then-owners of the so-called Onion River Land Company, brothers Ira, Ethan, Zimri and Heman Allen and their cousin Remember Baker. Ira Allen was appointed proprietors' clerk (the predecessor to the town clerk), and the politically savvy Colonel Thomas Chittenden served as the secretary. During that meeting, the group actually acknowledged that Burlington was part of New York but noted that considerable expense had been invested by the aforementioned company to clear a road from Castleton to Burlington and cultivate, improve and settle 1,500 acres along the Winooski River. They also voted themselves the right to each personally claim 103 acres to "pitch" (i.e., set up) a homestead, roads and other improvements.

The first proprietors' meeting adjourned, intending to meet again the following year at "Fortfradreck" in Colchester (referring to Ira Allen's Fort Frederick, a log blockhouse that sat beside the river in today's Winooski). That meeting would never come to fruition. In 1775, advancing redcoat raids scattered the early settlers southward. Ira's settlement near the river, at the present location of the Winooski roundabout, was burned. Nonetheless, the Onion River Company owned 70 percent of Burlington's acreage. The company was land rich and cash poor and had plenty of other landholdings all over the state. This narrowly focused investment strategy would come back to haunt the company. But the exodus into Burlington had begun.

The first settler to "pitch" in the Burlington town limits was Felix Powell, who bought today's Appletree Point and adjoining land to the north almost to the Winooski River. Powell came from Dorset, Vermont, and formerly hailed from Litchfield, Connecticut, the Allens' original hometown. He built a log cabin on the west shore of the point in the early 1770s and lived there for a few years. After leaving in 1775 for a couple of years during war raids, he sold his Burlington property to a man named James Murdock and moved south to Manchester, Vermont, in 1778. By then, Vermont had declared its independence from New York and New Hampshire and was engaged in the war, as well as British-led raids on settlements all over present-day Vermont. Northern Vermont was still a dangerous place to live.

Many other Vermont towns were settled with one thousand or more inhabitants before Burlington was populated, and for good reasons. In 1780, Governor Chittenden warned Vermont settlers that there would be no protection for Vermonters living north of Castleton. British-led raids on towns were still a constant threat, so picket forts or blockhouses had been built in Rutland, Pittsford, Castleton, Royalton and other towns near the latitude of the present Route 4. After 1780, a truce was negotiated between the northern British army and Vermont. This slowed down the frequency of attacks and gave settlers some breathing room and even resulted in prisoner exchanges. But that's a whole other story. Settlers kept streaming into Vermont towns, eager to buy affordable land and set up homes.

By the mid-1780s, many southern towns had swelled to 1,000 or more residents. The 1790 census counted only 331 residents scattered across Burlington's vast area. And in that year, Vermont was still an independent territory, barred by New York's congressional delegation from being admitted as a state. Why did New York finally relent and vote to admit Vermont into the union? Vermont agreed to pay New York $30,000—a king's ransom in those days (pun intended)—to settle its land disputes. In 1791, Vermont was officially admitted as the fourteenth state. Forgotten Deerfield was the one that got away from New York. Bustling Burlington soon overtook Middlebury as Vermont's biggest population center. By 1865, Burlington was proclaimed by its first mayor to be the "Queen City of Vermont."

8

Down in the Valley

The last mile-thick continental ice sheet melted thirteen thousand years ago. When geologists look at the Champlain Valley, they see glacial remnants and ancient landforms—signs of large-scale weathering and erosion of nearby formerly Himalayan-scale mountains. They observe a cliffside rock layer overthrust, where older rock that was transported one hundred miles westward over younger rock and now sits exposed at Lone Rock Point near Burlington High School. Multicolored quarry rocks and glacial erratic boulders sit hulking in the woods and fields.

For millennia, the saline Champlain Sea submerged the Champlain Valley, then eventually drained, leaving behind woolly mammoths and saltwater whales embedded in the fertile soil and glacial till. The sixth great lake once ebbed at Burlington's hillside. Rivers carved the land and replenished the landscape and supported a vast, rich web of life. The raw wilderness served migratory and indigenous humans for most of those thirteen thousand years. And Burlington's living landscape stayed relatively the same until the arrival of the European settlers.

Today's topography looks quite different than it did in 1763, and there's geography all but invisible to our eyes. Would you believe the hillside landscape in Burlington included a thirty-foot-wide, fifteen-foot-deep gulley meandering roughly diagonally downhill from Riverside Avenue near Intervale Road, down to near Maple and Battery Streets on the waterfront? The accompanying image shows a mid-1800s map of the Vermont Central Railroad tracks in the ravine. The ravine pitched downhill, from the top center of the map southward and westward toward the lake at the time.

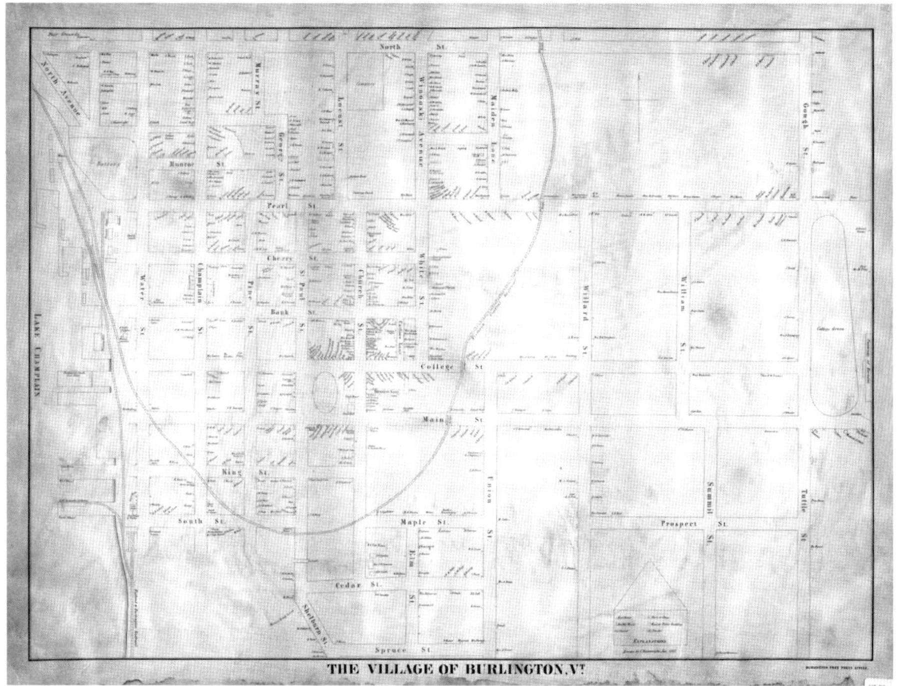

Vermont Central Railroad loop in the ravine during the mid-1800s. North, Pearl, College and Main Streets all had bridges over the ravine. *Silver Special Collections, UVM.*

The ravine was perhaps formed by an earlier meander of a much higher Winooski River, carved by water following the force of gravity and seeking its low point. The gully meandered across the city in an overall direction from north and east toward the south and west, creating a small valley on the surface of the land. As we know, water has the power to move and carry rocks, gravel, soil and sediments over great distances. Over hundreds and even thousands of years, water can significantly reshape the land. In this case, the sediments were deposited in the area where the water slowed and stopped: the lakeside. A small delta deposit was left in the area of what is now the railyard just to the south of Perkins Pier.

The early bayside colonial settlement was oriented as a grid and sloped down to the waterfront. But early development didn't happen on Burlington's hill section east of Winooski Avenue. There is a simple reason for the lack of early development on the hill. According to historian Hugo Martínez Cazón, as colonial settlers bought land and built farms and businesses in the town, the Burlington ravine presented a barrier to development. The hill section of the city was isolated from the downtown and waterfront.

The ravine was used as an aforementioned railway bed for a few decades. A temporary railroad station occupied the corner of Maple (then South) and St. Paul Streets before the waterfront depot and station were built. A track was laid in the ravine to move sawed lumber by train cars from the water-powered sawmills on the Winooski River down to the Burlington Harbor for shipping. As seen on the map, bridges carried people over the ravine on Main, College, North and Pearl Streets. Eventually, the track was moved out of the ravine and rerouted along the lakeside and through a tunnel under North Avenue. The tracks continued along the intervale and over the river to Winooski. The tunnel and river bridge still exist and are in use today.

During the winter, the original ravine and the hill became a sliding attraction. Sleds and toboggans were commonplace on the snowy slopes of the hill in the 1800s. During Burlington's short-lived winter carnival, according to Cazón, contestants would ride twelve-person toboggans, called traverses, from South Williams Street down Main Street to the lake, reaching speeds of up to sixty miles per hour. But in the late 1800s, the ravine became popular for other uses, too.

Early city dwellers had no organized way to discard waste. How could Burlington citizens discard garbage and sewage and avoid problems such as pools of human waste in the streets that plagued the larger cities in Europe and the Northeast colonies? It became common to toss trash over the hill, where it would be out of sight and out of mind. In some cases, it would become buried. And that's exactly what residents did. Hillsides tended to become dumping grounds for trash for decades. This included locations such as the northern edge of Riverside Avenue, the ravine that cut across the hill section and other slopes in the city.

As a result, the ravine was a convenient location to drain sewage away from living areas, and it officially became a public sewer. By the 1880s, when Burlington mushroomed with growth, the city had installed pipes, sluiceways and brick and stone culverts. The primitive wastewater effluent was partially or completely buried in the ravine, and it percolated downhill toward the lake near present-day Maple Street.

As the built environment became denser and the demand for usable space increased, the ravine was filled in with enormous quantities of wood shavings and sawdust from the mills, refuse or whatever was at hand. Old newspaper accounts describe the impact of the ravine and the extent of the problem it posed for navigating and building in the city. A September 7, 1886 column in the *Burlington Clipper* mentioned filling the ravine with old crockery, cans, dead animals, brush and sawdust. So much of the ravine was filled in that it gradually became less and less noticeable. The former bridges at North, Pearl, College and Main Streets were removed once the ravine was filled in underneath them. Today, the casual observer can notice the deep elevation of the Memorial Auditorium parking lot or the elevation drop at the intersection of Church and King Streets that reveals an inkling of the original topography.

However disguised the ravine became over time as it was filled in, the stability of the landscape as a foundational platform for buildings was still a ticking time bomb. Brick and mortar and wood structures were built on soil that was unstable and usually not compacted. Composting waste shrank in volume over time. And worse yet, shifting soil due to underground flowing water compromised buildings that were sitting on the surface.

According to Cazón, geologists say there is a high probability of a river flowing twenty to thirty feet below the surface of the ravine! When water moves through the soil, the soil particles tend to move as well. Gravity, being the universal force it is, enables whatever is underground to move as well. Over time, the movement produces instability for anything that is built on top of it.

One case that illustrates this is the shifting foundation of the Fletcher Free Library building, located on the corner of College Street and South Winooski Avenue. The massive brick and stone structure has suffered significant foundation problems as the unstable earth moves under it in a slow, continuous creep. Over time, the library foundation has required noteworthy structural renovations to keep it from being undermined. Likewise, the aging and presently condemned Memorial Auditorium next door to the library was built on the edge of the ravine and is in the same predicament.

But the geological and biological realities aren't the only impacts of the ravine. By the late 1800s, the ravine marked a social divide in the community. The commercial and industrial waterfront and less affluent sections of town along Battery Street and the neighborhoods around St. Joseph's Church were crowded with newer arrivals who hadn't yet established themselves.

As the ravine was filled in and the hillside acreage became more accessible, large, fashionable estates on ample lots began to create an upscale neighborhood. These were the handsome and stylish mansions of bankers and lumber and marble barons, with panoramic views and open land for gardens and orchards. The hill section was capped off with the evolving ivory towers of the university. In contrast, old newspaper articles talk about the higher crime rate in the "Bloody Third" Ward of the city, which was for a long time the site of some of the working-class neighborhoods.

Over time, many residents of the disadvantaged neighborhoods found success and moved to more affluent neighborhoods higher up the hill. They assimilated and intermarried or stayed and were sometimes displaced by commercial development. The ravine continued to be filled in over many years, and the geographic ethnic segregation became less apparent than in the past. Geologists continue to collect data and monitor the hidden ravine to better understand how to anticipate and minimize its impact on Burlington's built environment over time.

9

Twelve Millennia of Human History

Present-day Burlington's northern boundary is the ninety-mile-long Winooski River, a meandering highway of flotsam, jetsam and waterfalls on its way to Lake Champlain. From there, the water moves northward into the Richelieu River, the mighty St. Lawrence and, eventually, the Atlantic Ocean. The river's name is derived from the Abenaki word *winoskik*, meaning "at wild onion land." According to Abenaki (or Alnôbak) leaders, archaeological artifacts reveal that the area was inhabited by the original Native Americans, or Indians, for up to twelve thousand years before Europeans appeared and claimed it in the seventeenth century.

Native historians and archaeologists know a long and rich period of culture during those millennia that is often hidden from present-day light, especially for non-Natives. It is risky for an author of mainly European descent to attempt to narrate a Native American story. Even though this information may come from Abenaki sources, it is bound to be subjected to scrutiny. The author hopes this chapter will honor and preserve and not appropriate the narrative. Other cautions persist as well.

Within the Abenaki, there are debates over aspects of their language and history. Is it possible to give an accurate accounting of a history that survives on oral tradition, without a large body of written history to cite? How can one do justice to the story if anything that might be in dispute is edited out?

In an effort to honor and preserve the culture, the author has used Abenaki sources and asked some Abenaki friends to weigh in on this account for validity through the Abenaki lens. The author acknowledges his risk and proceeds with a short account of a long history that is best told by the elders.

Abenaki working at the Vermont Indigenous Heritage Center in Burlington. *Courtesy of the author.*

A while ago, Dr. Fred Wiseman, tribal member and the director of the Vermont Indigenous Heritage Center, described the long history, starting with the Abenaki ancestors ("the oldest ones") dating to the end of the last ice age, known as Adebaskedon ("the Years of the Mammoth"). The oldest ones were bound together by language and kinship and lived in dispersed groups of families. They hunted small and medium game with javelins and fished, following food sources on a yearly cycle.

Over thousands of years, the tundra slowly emerged from an ice world into a land of firs, willows and softwood and hardwood forests. This brought new game to the landscape, including *demakwa* (beaver), *awasos* (black bear), *beso* (lynx), *apanakega* (marten), *moskwas* (muskrat), *moz* (moose), *kokwa* (porcupine) and *meskagodagihla* (spruce grouse). The Native peoples' diets were supplemented with bark, berries, tubers and leaves.

A gradual warmer and drier period evolved for another few thousand years, known as the "Years of the Moose," from 10,000 to 6,500 years ago. Dense, tall woodlands followed with emerging warmer species, including butternut and white oak. More sophisticated stone-ground tools, such as the adze and gouge, were used to create dugout canoes, an improvement over skin-boats of the past. Bear, caribou, black bass, muskellunge, northern pike, salmon, sturgeon, yellow perch, blueberries, currants, raspberries and wild strawberries were also important parts of the peoples' diet. Bark containers were filled with cooked berries and maple sweetener, sealed with moose fat and hung from wigwam frames.

Dr. Wiseman described the next period, from 6,500 to 1,000 years ago, as a still warmer and wetter climate. There are many such village sites that have been found and studied in present-day Colchester and Burlington. Families and villages became larger and more complex. The people crafted wood using stone, metal and bone tools, which improved water travel and hunting. These ancestors of the Abenaki lived in clusters of wigwams. The wigwam was a conical frame of flexible saplings with birch, elm or softwood bark covering sewn to the frame with spruce roots.

The people (as Wiseman referred to them) perfected plant gathering and lived on a plant-dominated diet. Summers brought blueberries, elderberries, grapes and raspberries. The fall brought a stockpile of acorns, beechnuts, black walnuts, chestnuts, hazelnuts and hickory nuts. The plant diet was supplemented by upland hunting of bobcat, deer, fisher, partridge, red fox, turkey and porcupine. In the lowland, marsh hunting provided beaver, Canada geese, muskrat, otter and box turtle.

They honored their connection with the spiritual world in cycles of birth, death, dreams, spirit, sun, moon and seasons. The spirit worlds were interpreted by shamans and the clear-seers, or clairvoyants.

The people found advancements as trade expanded beyond Wôbanakik (the "Land of the Dawn" and today's northern New England area). Subsistence labor, which focused only on the local harvest, declined. People used time for crafting functional and ornamental objects such as stoneware and green mountain soapstone body ornaments. Beads, gorgets, pendants and whistles were crafted from metal, polished stone and shells. Clay cooking pots mark the end of this period.

The period from one thousand years ago up until European contact marked the advent of the bow and arrow and the introduction of agriculture. Crops included corn, red beans, kidney beans, summer squashes, Jerusalem artichokes, acorns and other nuts and tobacco. It also

Abenaki crafter at the Vermont Indigenous Heritage Center in Burlington. *Courtesy of the author.*

marked the loss of hunting lands to a new group of people from the south-central Appalachian area.

The Abenaki way of life was defined by the seasons. Spring began during the sugar-making moon of early spring. This occurred when sap began to flow in birch and maple trees. Crafting with bark to make canoes, dwellings and basketry were common in the spring. Summer was the hunting and gathering season, including planting, harvesting and playing games such as *adowiz* (a ring and pin game), *gagwenigan* (a dice game) and the oldest organized North American sport, lacrosse.

Fall was marked by the main hunting season, eel-fishing season and corn processing with a mortar. In winter, the hunters returned to the villages with animal harvests. This was a season of social renewal and games in wigwams and longhouses. Specialized winter clothing such as moose hide leggings, moccasins and snowshoes enhanced Alnôbak winter hunting. The Natives showed a reverence for the spirit world of plants and animals. They believed the plant and animal spirits offered themselves to be used by people for sustenance and survival. The spirit of Flint Mother was the origin of flint for making stone harvesting tools. In return, people needed to pay their respects and honor other living things through ceremonies.

Turbulent years erupted from 1600 to 1820 on the European calendar. Native coastal villagers were the first to come in contact with people from France. In exchange for information about the land and animals, the French gave glass beads, woven cloth and iron. Iron changed how the people of Wôbanakik interacted with nature; using iron needles, fishhooks, points, knives and axes proved more efficient than using chipped or ground stone tools. Rifles became common weapons along with tomahawks and traditional technology, and firearms became essential for survival.

Respect for conservation and game animals was challenged as hunting and trapping territories came under attack for commercial gain for beaver, deer and other game. A cycle of year-round war with other nations and the Europeans ensued; diseases and unfriendly visitors took their toll and decimated the Indian populations and the culture. But the Abenaki survived, and the people and culture are very much alive in the twenty-first century in Burlington and the rest of Vermont.

Today, the Vermont Indigenous Heritage Center on the intervale at the Ethan Allen Homestead Park offers artifact exhibits, tours and activities that allow us to appreciate the vibrant Alnôbak culture that inhabited the Burlington area for millennia, long before the Europeans arrived.

III

TICKETS TO RIDE

10

The Horse Ferry with No Name

Seldom is the 120-mile-long, 12-mile-wide Lake Champlain calm. The wind picks up at a moment's notice, and gusts howl and bluster through the valley between the Adirondacks and the Green Mountains something fierce. Over three hundred shipwrecks lie from one end of the lake to the other. Fate doomed at least a handful of ships that now rest on or near the floor of Burlington Bay. They include the sail-rigged canal boats *OJ Walker* and *General Butler* and the mysterious horse-powered ferry. The horse ferry sank in the 1840s; the *Walker* and *Butler* sank later in the century. Although there are no Spanish galleons to be found in Lake Champlain as far as we know, the three hulls remain as archaeological treasures and interesting recreational dive sites in less than one hundred feet of water.

Just north of the breakwater, eight fathoms down, lies an unusual wooden ship that is a whopping sixty-three feet long and twenty-three feet wide. This boat with no name is a unicorn, because it was equine-powered. At the time it sank, it was already a vanishing breed; even today, the horse ferry is almost forgotten and unknown to most people. To fathom what is submerged in the lake we need to understand the era. Boats powered by billowing sails and tired arms pulling oars were old and proven technologies of the eighteenth century. Nevertheless, water remained the preferred transportation mode for several reasons.

By 1800, very few paths in the Champlain Valley wilderness had been improved to be what we would consider even a logging road. Land travel in Vermont was slow and bone-rattling. Railroads existed in futuristic fantasies;

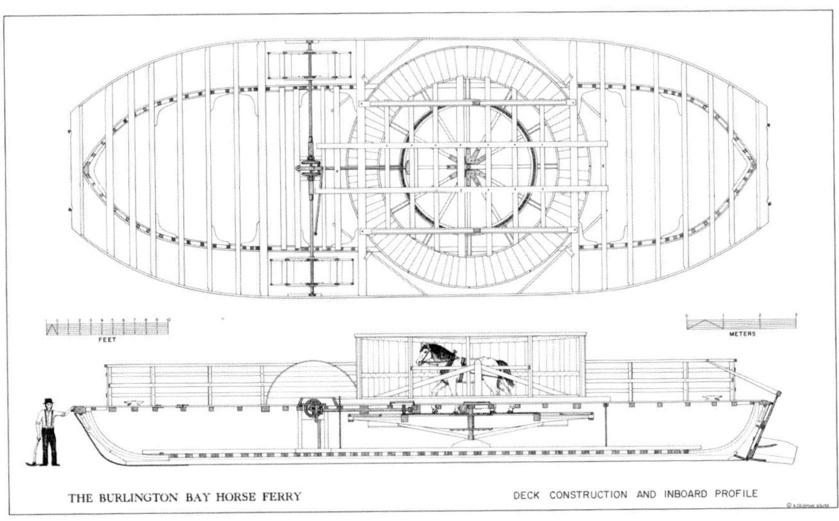

A sketch of the Burlington Bay horse ferry based on the archaeological survey. *Reconstruction by Kevin Crisman.*

its infrastructure and technology had yet to be built. Although the first steam-powered boats had been invented by 1807, it would be another decade or more before they were plentiful on the lake. For a couple of decades or more, horse-powered ferryboats for shorter trips across Lake Champlain were all the rage.

The horse ferries were wooden boats with circular, treadmill-like platforms mounted amidships. The energy from trotting horses turned a treadwheel and gear mechanism mounted on an axle to power two paddlewheels on the port and starboard sides of the boat.

Horse-powered ferries hauled passengers and cargo on the lake at nine different crossings throughout that era. They did best in the narrower parts of the lake with short crossings, not as long-haulers on the more dangerous twelve-mile broad crossings. The key horse ferry crossings we know the most about were from Chimney Point, Vermont, to Port Henry, New York; Basin Harbor, Vermont, to Westport, New York; Charlotte, Vermont, to Essex, New York; and limited operations in the Alburgh, Vermont area.

By the early 1800s, the ferries offered reliable water transportation and must have been considered a mechanical marvel, with the clip-clopping of hooves on hardwood planks and splashing side-wheelers churning through the lake water. The so-called horse boats, which could employ as many as six horses trotting head to tail on a circular treadwheel, were a cheaper alternative to steam-powered ships. Charlotte historian William Wallace Higbee, in portraying the boats, described the whip as fuel. The demand for speed simply required greater application of rawhide, especially in high winds and rough seas. Today, we can imagine the possibility that animal-rights advocates would have something to say about horse-powered ferries.

The first horse boat launched on the lake was the *Experiment,* with its maiden voyage in 1826. This boat was used at the two-mile crossing between Chimney Point and Port Henry. That crossing was one of the oldest routes and had been operating with sail ferries since 1785. The ruggedly built *Experiment* could hold six wagons with horses and other passengers and cargo. It made up to several round trips a day and used two horses to power the boat.

Another noteworthy two-horsepower boat was the *Eagle*, launched a few years later in 1832. It plied the prosperous Basin Harbor–Westport route across three and a half miles of water. Anyone familiar with that section of the lake knows that a lot can happen in those three miles. The towering Adirondack peaks, nearby sheer palisade cliffs, deep river valleys and the thermal mass of the lake can all factor into the magnitude and direction of winds and storms. Even without these dynamics, there is frequently unexpected mayhem on the water. The owners advertised the *Eagle* as a superior boat, and it made three round trips a day during the peak summer season, two a day during spring and fall and one round trip on Sundays. On a rough day with strong winds, two horses would have been pushed hard to pull that boat when it was loaded with cargo. Both the *Experiment* and the *Eagle* were similar in size at over sixty feet in length. There is no record of their eventual demise.

In 1828, businessmen Charles McNeil and Henry Ross launched the best-known horse ferry on Lake Champlain, named the *Eclipse*. It worked the three-mile Charlotte–Essex crossing. This route logged a similar distance as the Basin Harbor run but lay twelve miles to the north. The *Eclipse* held records as the longest and longest-running horse boat on the lake. It was sixty-eight feet long and twenty-five feet wide, with six horses pushing a horizontal treadwheel. Assembled at Shelburne Shipyard, the boat had a long life ferrying people, wagons, livestock and produce back and forth across the lake, and it reportedly made its owners wealthy. In midcareer, the *Eclipse* underwent a major refurbishing, as most horse boats did after ten years of service. But all good things must come to an end.

By 1847, the *Eclipse* was old and tired. On a trip from Essex with a load of cattle, its deck collapsed, treadwheel and all. The livestock and animals were forced to swim for it, and the decrepit hull was towed to a nearby sandy beach. And like the *Eclipse*, the horse-boat era didn't last long.

Unfortunately, the wreck known as the Burlington horse ferry is truly a boat with no name, which was not uncommon. After years of underwater surveys, nautical archaeologists Kevin Crisman and Art Cohn were unable to determine its identity or owners, but they did piece together some answers to a few perplexing questions. Although the Burlington boat was similar to the *Eclipse*, the researchers ruled it out as the Burlington horse ferry.

The remains of the Burlington horse ferry include most of the intact hull, including planks, gears, axles, rudder and paddle wheels. The gears and axle were made of mold-poured iron, while the axle bushings were composed of copper alloys, which would have diminished dangerous friction of the high-rpm, metal-on-metal contact. The wood treadwheel is where the other wear and tear happened.

Typically, treadwheel planks were composed of hardwood, as was the hull. And when treadmill planks broke, the horse's foot often broke through the fatigued plank. In this catastrophic situation, a heavy beast trotting on the wheel could break a leg. The end result became an unpleasant experience for everyone. As such, in an attempt to reduce the risk of catastrophic failure, the planks were most likely replaced often. And the ferrymen often employed smaller, lighter horses in an attempt to reduce wear and eventual failure.

In the case of the Burlington horse ferry, smaller horses were indeed used, as determined by the size 00 horseshoes found onboard. A large number of broken horseshoes and leather harness pieces stashed in the hold of the hull also indicated that the operators were most likely running a shoestring operation, reusing and cobbing together old parts if they could. The hull was fashioned of red oak, which was cheaper but more susceptible to rot than white oak. Even though all oak is hardwood, the use of the lesser red oak may have indicated the owners' attempt to cut costs or a lack of availability. No living quarters were found on board, as with some horse ferries, but a broken pottery tea or coffee pot was found, and a seed collection including black cherries, black walnuts, beechnuts, hickory nuts and wild plums suggested a diet.

Several discoveries fuel conjecture that the boat was intentionally scuttled. First, a hole appeared to have been punched through the hull below the waterline. Parts of the boat, including the rudder, had been stashed in the bow of the boat. After ten to twenty years of service, the boat might have been towed to Burlington for repairs or to sell and later scuttled.

Seldom was there any public notice of scuttling boats, except in the case of a fatality or serious accident. Crisman and Cohn believe the most likely candidates for the identity of the Burlington horse ferry may be the Basin Harbor *Eagle* or the Chimney Point *Experiment*. Both boats began service around the same time and were replaced with new boats in the 1840s. This archaeological treasure may be the *Experiment*, the *Eagle* or another boat altogether. As of this writing, only the lake knows for sure.

11

The Storm of the Century

Captain William Montgomery of Isle La Motte was the third owner of the *General Butler*, a schooner-rigged, eighty-eight-foot-long canal boat that he piloted on Lake Champlain. The thirty-seven-year-old captain, who had been born in New Brunswick, was no rookie pilot on the lake. During the 1860s, he built a house on Main Street in Isle La Motte, the northernmost island on the lake. On the island, nearby marble (limestone) quarries offered Montgomery a lifetime of shipping opportunities for a schooner captain. He had piloted ships loaded with marble and other products for decades.

At only fourteen feet wide, the narrow *General Butler*, which had been built in Essex, New York, was suitable for hauling heavy loads through the narrow canals to the populated commercial centers at either end of the lake. By 1876, it was showing its fourteen-year-old age, but it was far from being washed up. On December 9, the schooner was loaded with some thirty tons of black marble from Fisk Quarry on the west shore of Isle La Motte, headed for Burlington. In addition to being a shipping port, Burlington had at least two stone-cutting marble mills in that era.

Onboard the *General Butler* with Montgomery was an unnamed crew member and Elisha Goodsell, who was an Isle La Motte quarry operator. Goodsell had recently suffered an eye injury and was planning to see the doctor that day. To complete the manifest, Captain Montgomery's fifteen-year old daughter, Cora, and her girlfriend tagged along for their first ride on the ship with plans to do Christmas shopping at some establishments in Burlington.

Canal schooner replica *Lois McClure*, built at the Lake Champlain Maritime Museum. It is similar to freight-hauling canal boats in the nineteenth century. *Courtesy of the author.*

The long canal boats were trusty ships in their day, capable of hauling heavy cargoes up and down the lake, dropping their masts and being towed through the canals. The ships typically hoisted gaff-rigged sails and were well-built and adept vessels in good to fair weather. Most of the canal boats during the heyday of lake shipping followed a similar design and dimensions. A wood or coal stove-heated cabin, with windows in the stern, offered bunks and cozy living space. Some captains lived aboard their boats with their families for years at a time.

Quite often, the shallower northern reaches of the lake near Isle La Motte ice up or become frozen solid in December. Captain Montgomery hoped to squeeze in an easy run to Burlington late in the season. As historian Art Cohn says, the fact that Montgomery was sailing that late in the season tells us something. That is, he felt it was a necessity to be out there. We can only speculate whether it was to complete a contract, make extra money or another reason. Little did he know what the lake had in store for them that day.

As Lake Champlain boaters know, conditions can change instantly; in fifteen minutes, the lake can go from placid to perilous. A forty-mile trip could take a few hours in an obstacle course around reefs that would leave little room for mistakes. We know that Captain Montgomery and his crew had no prior warning of what they were sailing into or what was about to befall them. Once they were underway, a strong wind, rolling swells and snow pelted the ship. As soon as the ship entered the broad lake, south of the island, the fetch over open water would amplify the waves.

The winds became alarming. Snow and freezing spray collected on tattered rigging, and waves coated the deck. Normally gritty with dirt from the quarry rock, the decking became a treacherous sheet of ice. The dangerous gale-force winds and enormous waves of a one-hundred-year storm engulfed the ship. It pitched and yawed as it approached the relatively safer conditions inside Burlington Bay, where a protective breakwater had been constructed decades before of the same limestone blocks Montgomery was hauling.

Then it happened: the steering mechanism snapped. The intense stress of the wind and eight-foot swells pounding the ship in what witnesses said were below-zero temperatures were pushing the ship beyond its limits. Montgomery was powerless to control his disabled ship outside the breakwater. The passengers and crew were at the mercy of the relentless fury of the waves and wind.

Captain Montgomery ordered his crewman to throw off the storm anchor in an attempt to keep the ship from being demolished on the breakwater wall. They tried to jury rig the steering to get control. As the boat was relentlessly pounded while adrift outside the breakwater, they desperately wrapped a chain around the tiller bar and steering mechanism. Montgomery's last-ditch hope was to pull the anchor and aim the ship on a path to carry it around the south end of the breakwater. That would perhaps allow them one chance of getting closer to the safety of a wharf or into shore. Unable to retrieve the anchor, which was hooked on the bottom of the lake, the crewman climbed into the bow and cut the anchor line with an axe. The liberated boat missed clearing the breakwater, and the bow slammed onto the top of the immovable wall of boulders.

Eyewitnesses on shore watched as the waves lifted the heavy wooden ship out of the water and slammed it onto the breakwater, only for the vessel to slide back down into a trough and be picked up again and smashed onto the breakwater by another wall of water. Captain Montgomery realized it wouldn't be long before the rocks would bash a hole through the hull and the ship instantly sink into the depths. We can imagine Cora and her girlfriend hanging on in the sheltered cabin, praying for a miracle. There Montgomery was, at the mercy of the waves, with the girls, Goodsell and the crewman, seeing only one possible option left for survival.

When the walloping waves lifted the ship and slammed it onto the breakwater, Montgomery helped his two female passengers jump off gingerly onto the icy rocks of the breakwater, one at a time. Then he helped his crewman. Then Goodsell jumped off. He slipped and struck his head and lay unconscious on the icy rocks. Finally, Captain Montgomery jumped off the ship as it slipped back into the lake and sank, seventy-five yards west of the breakwater and forty feet beneath the surface.

All five in the party would have succumbed to hypothermia right there on the breakwater had it not been for a local hero. James Wakefield, a ship chandler with a sail and rigging shop, could see what was happening from his business (where the Shanty on the Shore restaurant is today on Battery Street). With dozens of curious spectators watching from the shoreline, Wakefield took matters into his own hands. He commandeered a fourteen-foot lighthouse service boat with the help of his fourteen-year-old son and rowed out to rescue the five souls from the breakwater.

Montgomery lowered his daughter and her friend into the waiting hands of Wakefield. The three men managed to precariously get themselves into the overloaded small boat. The five survivors were taken to a house on Battery Street and examined by Burlington doctor H.H. Langdon.

Once Cora Montgomery recovered from hypothermia and exhaustion, she asked if she could make the return trip home to Isle La Motte on the *General Butler* after it had been raised. The masts and rigging were recovered soon after the incident, but the marble-laden hull still rests on the bottom, a couple of hundred feet from the southwest end of the breakwater. Today, the *General Butler*, marked with a buoy, is a recreational dive site in Burlington Bay. Captain Montgomery lived to ship cargo to Europe, Brazil and other ports all over the world. He died in Isle La Motte at the age of ninety-one.

Almost twenty years later, on May 11, 1895, another canal boat was faced with similar wrath from the lake and elements. The *OJ Walker* was an eighty-six-foot-long canal boat with an almost unheard-of thirty-three-year history on Lake Champlain. The *Walker*'s captain, W.J. Worthen, was caught off guard just outside Burlington's breakwater. Worthen knew full well the story of the *General Butler*'s demise and the narrow escape of Captain Montgomery, his passengers and crew. The aging *OJ Walker*'s hull was wearing thin, and so was its luck. In a surprise spring storm, the boat, which was heavily loaded with brick and tile and on its way to the Shelburne estate of Dr. William Seward Webb, sprang a catastrophic leak. At a quarter-mile northwest of the breakwater, the *Walker* began filling with thirty-five-degree water and listing to one side.

Captain Worthen knew that the loaded ship would sink like a stone. He had just enough time to get his wife, a crewman and himself into a rowboat before the *OJ Walker* submerged in sixty-five feet of water. Regrettably, the rowboat had no oars. Fortunately for the intrepid sailors, a west wind carried them safely toward the Burlington shoreline in what must have felt like a never-ending ride. We can only imagine Worthen's relief of trading his boat and cargo for the opportunity to live another day. The *OJ Walker* rests in the silt today as another recreational dive site just outside and north of the breakwater.

12

From Buggies to Bobbers to Buses

In 1790, there were only seven houses within today's Burlington city limits. The rest were scattered on the outskirts in remote areas. The original town of Burlington sprawled over an area three times bigger than today, including present-day South Burlington, Williston and even Richmond. Burlington's business growth exploded in the next fifty years, along the waterfront, in the emerging Church Street business district and across town in the riverfront commercial district. Over the next few decades, the population would swell in the center as well. Burlington became a more centralized town of four thousand by 1840. If you wanted to get around Burlington, you had limited choices: on foot, on horseback, in a horse-drawn two-wheel buggy or by carriage, stage or wagon. The early paths and roads were often at best gravel paths that wound around boulders and outcroppings and followed higher and drier ground.

Railroads had appeared in the city during the 1840s, but they had a limited capacity for moving people within the local area. Many of the roads were private, and the builders charged a toll to use them. There was a growing demand to get around in Burlington, to Winooski mills across the river and out to Essex. The prospect and expense of travel around town were unappealing enough that horse-drawn omnibuses began to appear in the 1870s. The Winooski and Burlington Horse Railroad Company (WBHRRC) was established in 1872, offering horse-drawn trolley cars on rails to move people short distances. In 1885, the routes expanded from Shelburne Street to Burlington to Winooski. Other routes in fourteen-passenger trolley cars followed. The trolleys were equipped with a clonking horn to warn pedestrians and a cowcatcher bumper to clear the tracks. Since the wheelbase was short, the ends of the cars bobbed and see-sawed, hence the trolleys were commonly called "bobbers."

But the big cities were way ahead of Burlington and had been using trolleys powered by electric motors for a couple of decades. It is interesting to note that Vermonter Thomas Davenport invented the first electric motor in 1834. He used his small motor to power a toy car at that time. Politically connected inventors capitalized on his device and created the first full-scale electric locomotive in 1851, the year Davenport died.

It took a few decades for the electric trolley concept to ramp up to full-scale production. In 1893, the trolley company invested in the new electric infrastructure in what it believed would be more economical and faster service.

Enter John J. Flynn, one of the most influential giants in Burlington's history and an electric trolley pioneer. Flynn grew up dirt poor in Dorset, Vermont, and started out as a dairy farmhand, then worked his way up to farm manager. Once in Burlington, he found a business partner and formed

Burlington horse-drawn trolley, 1885. *Silver Special Collections, UVM.*

a grocery business. Another turning point in his life was marrying Nellie Wait and flipping almost thirty thousand acres in her hometown of Peru, Vermont. He made a fortune in real estate, and once he came to Burlington, he caught the attention of and formed partnerships with several other enterprising businessmen.

Flynn converted from his family's Catholic faith to Nellie's Protestant church and quickly fit in with the Burlington Yankee elite. He brought a confident and aggressive style and was involved with commercial, industrial and residential real estate transactions all over the city. His timing was perfect. The economy boomed, and real estate values accelerated. He owned several trolley companies in different Vermont towns and bought up electric companies to power them. When his Military Post Railway (MPR) ran into competition for infrastructure with Central Vermont Railway (CVR), his business partners got cold feet and sold their interests to him at a discount. Flynn wanted to run his trolleys from Winooski to Essex, but CVR denied him access to its tracks. He seems to have exemplified the old saying, "When the going gets tough, the tough get going!"

Fearing Flynn would interfere with its tracks on Main Street in Winooski, CVR placed guards at each end of the Winooski line. In response, Flynn hired a large crew of railway workers from Massachusetts and camped them out near the overpass in question. What happened next sounds like a scene out of a handbook of dirty tricks.

At midnight on a Saturday night, Flynn turned his workers loose, laying his new tracks on the overpass. The CVR guards were overwhelmed and backed down. Filing a court injunction was impossible on a Sunday morning, and the job was quickly done. Flynn's MPR began twenty-four-mile round trips from Winooski to Essex. Flynn then acquired the WBHRRC from an out-of-state absentee owner, and it became the Burlington Traction Company (BTC) in 1896.

At then-breakneck speeds of twenty-five to thirty miles per hour, the electric trolleys whizzed along twenty-minute routes. The BTC and other trolley ventures became prosperous. Thomas Davenport wouldn't have been surprised. Trolley transport offered indispensable routes to outlying towns and links with railroad transportation to the big cities. The trolleys brought commuters and customers into the city from the suburbs and helped support department stores and businesses in a thriving downtown.

As soon as electric trolleys became popular in Burlington, they began to pop up in other municipalities around the state, including Rutland, Bennington, Barre, Montpelier, Brattleboro, Bellows Falls, Fair Haven,

Poultney, Lake Bomoseen, Springfield, Waterbury and Stowe. Wild stories were told, such as the account of the trolley racing a railroad train, neck and neck on parallel tracks in St. Albans, and then derailing on a white-knuckle ride. Pranksters left blasting caps to explode under the wheels on the trolley tracks in Barre. It seemed that trolleys were everywhere and part of the culture.

The electric trolleys didn't spark overwhelming support at first. Some people railed about the exorbitant five-cent fare, and others feared trolleys were unsafe. And the trolleys had trouble on hills, of which there are plenty in the Queen City. Mechanical problems persisted, making service unpredictable at times.

The trolleys were popular and profitable for a while. But higher wages and city control over routes and fares eventually put a squeeze on profits and contributed to the BTC sliding into the red. Furthermore, the advent and production of cars and buses were pushing a giant paradigm shift that not everyone envisioned. A new transportation mode slowly but surely caught the attention of everyone, even Flynn.

In the early 1920s, a young competitor by the name of Bill Appleyard arrived on the scene . Appleyard was a Dartmouth graduate and had worked in the Texas oilfields and at a Massachusetts car dealership. He opened his own Dodge dealership in Burlington, Appleyard Motor Company. He also founded the Burlington Rapid Transit Company (BRTC), establishing bus lines that competed with the BTC.

Unfortunately, the November 1927 flood washed away the Winooski River bridge and hopes for Burlington's continued trolley routes across the river. But an even bigger force swamped the BTC for good. Gasoline-powered buses and automobiles, which offered personalized transportation and freedom, were the next big thing. And apparently Burlingtonians, like the rest of Americans, were ready for the change, as evidenced by what happened a couple of years later. Flynn wisely sold the BTC in 1929 to Appleyard. Flynn was already diversified in real estate, and he founded the Chittenden Trust Company, the forerunner of today's People's United Bank. But it was a time of unusual economic uncertainty, and it was about to get worse. Little did anyone know, the stock market crash and the Great Depression were only months away in October.

Appleyard was about to turn the corner on a transportation revolution, propelled by the spinning wheels of his bus company and car dealership. He had bought the BTC in March 1929, and he was a master marketer. He announced and advertised that the last day of the trolley service in Burlington

The August 4, 1929 trolley celebration on Main Street next to City Hall Park. Unknown photographer, probably taken from the hotel on Main Street. *Silver Special Collections, UVM.*

would be August 4 of that year, and to commemorate the occasion there would be a festive celebration.

After weeks of hype, more than five thousand enthusiastic people crowded into City Hall Park and Main Street to see the spectacle. The mob watched a funeral procession of mourners dressed in black, a dirge-playing military band, a bugler blowing "Taps" and a black-draped trolley car decorated with flowers being towed by a truck down Main Street.

The trolley car stopped at the park in the middle of Main Street. Dignitaries sat on the balcony of the nearby hotel across the street and watched, overlooking the spectacle and the throngs of bystanders at the scene. Burlington's "last" trolley car was then soaked with gasoline by two men and torched. It roared into towering flames as the crowd cheered. This stunt may seem unbelievable today, when even a backyard campfire is a no-no. The trolley era officially went up in flames and plumes of acrid black smoke.

The ceremony culminated with twenty of Appleyard's rubber-tired buses rolling down Main Street two abreast, turning and lining up outside City Hall Park to more cheers from the crowd. A few trolleys would continue service on the tracks for a few years, but the era was over. Just like the horse and buggy, the electric trolley quickly became hidden in the past.

13

The Sinkable Floating Museum

Steamboats replaced horse boats and sailboats and proliferated on the lake in the 1800s and continued to serve passengers into the 1900s. One of the last steam engine-powered ferries to make regular runs on the lake that is still preserved today was the *Ticonderoga*, a 220-foot beauty owned by the Champlain Transportation Company (CTC). Old-timers who rode on the vessel remembered the loud, timpani-like drumming of the huge pistons driven by the steam engine as the side-mounted paddle wheel churned through the lake on its excursions. As automobiles came on the scene in the 1920s and '30s, the *Ticonderoga* and other steamers began to ferry not only passengers but also up to twenty cars across the lake from Burlington to Port Kent, New York.

The lake transportation business was booming, and there was no shortage of ambitious men looking to capitalize on the demand for travel. One of them was Elisha N. Goodsell from the aforementioned lakeside town of Isle La Motte. Goodsell was the son of Elisha R. Goodsell, the survivor of the *General Butler* disaster. The younger Goodsell was no rookie in the shipping business. After graduating from high school in Plattsburgh, New York, and living on a farm in Alburgh, he took to the shipping business. He ferried people at three crossings in the Champlain Islands and served as a state senator and later as a representative. He also shipped limestone, which was called marble at the time, for the Burlington breakwater and other projects and for a marble-cutting company in Burlington. The Isle La Motte black marble was cut, polished and installed in swanky places like Radio City

The *Ticonderoga*, a passenger boat and later a car ferry, now preserved at the Shelburne Museum, seen in a 1934 image from a postcard. *Louis L. McAllister, Silver Special Collections, UVM.*

Music Hall in New York, the Vermont Statehouse and the National Gallery of Art in Washington, D.C., to name a few.

But competing with the CTC in 1923, which had been in business for almost a century, was a formidable endeavor. In order to compete with the big dogs, Captain Goodsell would have to build his own ferry docks that would hold up to auto traffic. He decided to use Port Douglas for the New York landing, instead of Port Kent, where the CTC dock was located. Goodsell bought a boat named the *Admiral* and retrofitted it to hold about fifteen cars. He drove pilings and built plank ramps for cars in Burlington. But the *Admiral* inexplicably sank at the dock, not once, but on a second occasion as well.

Captain Goodsell persevered and bought a second boat, the *Legonia*, in 1926 and kept his bow pointed into the wind. He pushed his luck by running his ferries for longer days and earlier and later in the season than the competition. He was the underdog, since his boats were smaller and less luxurious than the CTC boats, and his customers had to remain in their cars on the hour-long crossing because of lack of space. Nonetheless, he was rewarded with about 40 percent of the traffic of the twenty-five thousand cars that crossed the lake in 1926.

In 1929, the Champlain Bridge was built between Chimney Point and Crown Point, New York, which drained away some ferry business. Goodsell had also built a "vertical lift" toll bridge over the span from Rouses Point to Alburgh at about the same time. Using a pulley system, the center of the bridge could be lifted to accommodate ship masts passing underneath. His fleet of ferries out of Burlington continued to feed his cash flow. Goodsell was always looking for another way to capitalize and innovate, and his ambition fueled his next move.

At that time, the world's super-rich sailed big pleasure yachts on the high seas. One such example was the *Oneida*, a five-hundred-gross-ton, two-hundred-foot-long steel-hulled steam yacht built in 1897. The *Oneida* had been owned by a couple of different wealthy bankers and, later, by William Randolph Hearst, one of the greatest media moguls in the world. The *Oneida* had been refurbished with new oil boilers, fed by a thirty-eight-thousand-gallon fuel capacity that boasted a four-thousand-mile seagoing range. For several years, Hearst sailed the *Oneida* to distant ports, from Tahiti to the Mediterranean, up the Amazon River, through the Panama Canal and up the Pacific coast.

In 1917, the *Oneida* was commissioned for military service by the U.S. government as *SP-432* for a few months, but it never saw military action. After that, the yacht was used for motion pictures and pleasure cruises for celebrity friends and was docked at the Hearst Castle in the village of San Simeon, California. It was outfitted with luxury accommodations for Hearst and his secretary, with a separate bedroom for his wife. The staterooms were complemented with ivory and gold fixtures and resplendent in mahogany furnishings, crimson damask hangings and soft, plush bedding. But a cloud of intrigue surrounded the ship. During the time Hearst owned the *Oneida*, it was the center of an inquiry into a high-profile, suspicious and unexplained death. This occurred after a movie star named Thomas H. Ince spent a weekend on the vessel in 1924.

Ince was a big-time screenwriter, producer and actor who made over eight hundred films. He was called the "father of the Western" and even built his own independent studios. Ince and Hearst were negotiating a movie deal, and Hearst had invited Ince to celebrate his birthday aboard the *Oneida*. While staying on the boat, Ince suffered an attack, either from food or heart problems. Conflicting accounts fueled rampant rumors after Ince died a few days later at the age of forty-four. Gossip brewed about jealousy, poisoning, a shooting and hush money; and the rumors persisted for years. Hearst, who had become rich by peddling yellow journalism, was now the object of relentless sensationalized rumors. Although no charges were ever filed, Hearst never lived down the suspicions and questions surrounding the actor's death. The incident inspired a 2001 motion picture, *The Cat's Meow*, about the mystery of Ince's demise.

The *Admiral* and *Oneida* at anchor at the Burlington dock, January 9, 1934. *Louis L. McAllister, Silver Special Collections, UVM.*

In 1932, Hearst sold the yacht at a bargain price to none other than Captain Elisha N. Goodsell. Goodsell retrofitted the *Oneida* in Newburg, New York, on the Hudson River to accommodate autos and removed the two masts while keeping the luxurious accommodations intact. He sold an accessory speedboat and then reportedly sailed the ship up the Atlantic coast, then down the St. Lawrence River, through the canals on the Richelieu River to Lake Champlain. But navigating a twenty-four-foot-wide ocean liner with an eleven-foot draft into Burlington Bay and running a route to Valcour, New York, created new challenges. The *Oneida*'s deeper draft required dredging and building new ramps and a new pier in Valcour, at the very least.

The *Oneida* could hold seventy-five cars at once. For a dime, visitors could descend into the former Hearst living quarters and behold the opulent splendor that had been preserved as a museum. Postcards sold for another dime, which was equivalent to a couple of dollars in today's money.

But the ills of the Great Depression churned into the ferry profits along with bridges and competition. Goodsell's main competitor, the CTC, which by then was owned by the Delaware and Hudson Railroad, was taking a financial hit and was additionally being impacted by Goodsell's ferries and the Vermont–New York bridges at either end of the lake. It's unclear exactly how long the *Oneida* served customers on Lake Champlain in those years, and Goodsell faced mounting problems. For one, he didn't maintain his ramps and piers very well.

In 1931, a truck crashed through a Goodsell ramp, and the Burlington aldermen required him to make repairs to his facilities, which were in deplorable appearance and condition. Goodsell ignored the city's demands and continued doing business. At the insistence of the city, Goodsell posted liability bonds but persisted in using his ramshackle docks and ramps despite city complaints. At that point, the city wanted Goodsell to leave so they could build a new pier using Works Progress Administration funding.

In 1934, unusually high lake levels and ice demolished Goodsell's Burlington ramps once and for all. Although he promised to rebuild them, he finally threw in the towel once his enterprise sank to new lows. Until that time, all three of his original boats—the *Admiral*, *Legonia* and *Oneida*—were still in service. The *Admiral* was still hauling black marble from Isle La Motte to Burlington. But in 1937, the *Burlington Free Press* reported that the *Legonia* and *Oneida* were being stripped in preparation for being scrapped.

The three vessels were tied up at a dock for several years, and by 1939, all three of the Goodsell ferries were lying partially submerged in the industrialized Burlington harbor, a vexation to city officials and others. A drive to clean up the waterfront put pressure on Goodsell and others to remove the wrecks from the bay, both in and on the water and harborside. The Goodsell ferries and other sunken ships were raised.

The city was ready to tow the *Oneida* into deep water and sink it when a buyer appeared at the eleventh hour and towed the vessel to St. John, Quebec. But the rusting hull proved the ferry wasn't unsinkable. It barely made it over the Canadian border, and it submerged again. Eventually, the hull was hauled out and cut up in St. John, Quebec, and sold for scrap by a Canadian munitions firm.

In 1897, the *Oneida* had cost $1,250,000 to build and retrofit. It was sold as scrap iron for $40 in 1940. The ever-colorful Elisha N. Goodsell continued to operate a ferry between Fort Ticonderoga and Larrabee Point until his death at age eighty-seven in 1960. A cable ferry operates near the same location today.

IV

ARCHITECTURAL RICHES

14

Age Before Beauty

Anyone who has set foot in Burlington cannot help but notice the large number of spectacular mansions that were built in the late nineteenth and early twentieth centuries. A handful of those buildings are profiled in the coming chapters as representatives of a vast collection. But Burlington also has an elite group of even older surviving buildings that were erected between 1785 and 1800. All of them arose during the first generation of Burlington wood-frame homes. Unlike the architectural beauty contest of the ensuing grand mansions, these homes were more utilitarian and less architecturally stunning. The early buildings were smaller in scale than the later mansions, and generally, their inhabitants lived in close quarters. Often, the families included eight or more children and sometimes extended family members in these homes. Although not all historians are unanimous on this list or the credentials, the following five, and possibly one or two more, belong to this eighteenth-century age-before-beauty club.

The Ethan Allen House

The earliest surviving building is plausibly the Ethan Allen Homestead, where General Allen lived with Fanny, their children and two servants. Several

Left: The Ethan Allen Homestead in Burlington, near the Winooski River. *Courtesy of the author.*

Opposite: The Colonel Stephen Pearl House on Pearl Street. *Courtesy of the author.*

prominent Vermont historians have concluded that the preponderance of evidence supports the belief that this one-and-a-half-story house, sited on the Burlington intervale, was commissioned by General Allen and built by his brother Ira before 1787, when the Allen family moved in. The family added barns and outbuildings while they lived there. After the Allens left, it was subsequently renovated and expanded and continued to be used as a farmhouse in the centuries that followed. The house has been restored to its near-original integrity. The Ethan Allen Homestead Museum sits in the Winooski Valley Park District near the Winooski River.

THE PEARL HOUSE

Two years later, after General Allen died in 1789, a five-by-two-bay home on a rubble foundation was built by Frederick Saxton at what is now 12 Colchester Avenue. Except for the dormers and back additions, the main body of the hip-roof home is original. In 1794, the building and fifty acres of the surrounding forest were sold to Revolutionary War veteran Colonel Stephen Pearl, a survivor of the Battle of Bunker Hill. He was remembered

as an amiable public servant in his employment as sheriff, justice of the peace, tax collector and other roles. Pearl and his wife entertained in the house, which was one of only a few buildings on the path from the East End river mills to the bay. The "road to Pearl's house" became Pearl Street in Burlington's early years. After the Pearls departed, other high-profile Burlingtonians owned the home. In 1919, it was sold to UVM.

THE POMEROY HOUSE

Dr. John Pomeroy practiced medicine in Cambridge, Vermont, before moving to Burlington in 1792, where he lived in a log cabin for a couple of years. The Pomeroy House, which he built in 1796 at 166 Battery Street, was his home and office. Pomeroy was one of Burlington's early medical doctors and a professor of medicine at UVM. In the decades that followed, he trained apprentices and held classes in his house. After Pomeroy died in the house in 1844, it was sold and later used as a boardinghouse for laborers. It was eventually saved as part of the renovation project of the historic Holloway Block in 1981.

Top: The Dr. John Pomeroy House on Battery Street. *Courtesy of the author.*

Middle: The Converse Home on lower Church Street. *Courtesy of the author.*

Bottom: The Horace Loomis House on Pearl Street. *Courtesy of the author.*

The Converse Home

The Converse Home at what is now number 272 at the lower end of Church Street was originally a five-bay Federal-style home built in 1799 by William Chase Harrington. It boasted a stunning view of the lake and was surrounded by an eighty-acre farm. While Harrington lived there, it was the site of the first UVM trustee meetings, before there was a main UVM building. Harrington served as an assemblyman, UVM trustee and the state's attorney who prosecuted Cyrus Dean and others in the Black Snake Affair. The building is named after John K. Converse, who bought the then-sprawling building for his family in 1844 and also established the Burlington Female Seminary and, later, a home for older women. The Converse Home has served as an assisted-living community since that time.

The Horace Loomis House

The Horace Loomis House at 342 Pearl Street was built in 1800 by Loomis, a son of the aforementioned Phineas Loomis, who had entertained Prince Edward at his home across the road five years earlier. This Federal-style home has seen porches and rooms added over the centuries. Loomis, who continued his father's tannery business, was a Burlington socialite and at one time entertained Secretary of State Henry Clay and President William Henry Harrison, among other notables. This building remained a social center in Burlington from the time of its construction until it was recently sold again.

15
The Mansion on the Hill

If you ask a Burlingtonian to name three of the most architecturally impressive buildings, you are likely to get a dozen answers. Why is Burlington filled with so much alluring architectural eye candy? The inspiring styles usually followed from the good fortunes of local and transplanted tycoons, ship captains, merchants and thriving professionals who built their mansions beginning in the early shipyard days and through the century that followed. Some of the credit points to a handful of talented architects with names like John Johnson, Ammi B. Young, Walter Dickson, J.J. Randall and Henry Hobson Richardson. Of course, some of the mansions were lost to the ages, but we will focus on those that are still with us today.

Picking favorites from all of these beauties is a daunting task. By popular acclaim, we have narrowed our gaze to five nineteenth-century buildings that represent great design, craftsmanship and stories: Grasse Mount, where the Marquis de Lafayette wined and dined during his visit to Burlington in 1825; the French chateau–style Richardson Building, which anchors Church Street; the last of the great waterfront mansions, the Greek Revival–style Follett House; the Old Mill, which sprung from the original UVM building; and the Billings Library at UVM. The author snuck in a couple of bonus selections, at his discretion. This chapter, and the four that follow, will describe these architectural monuments.

Grasse Mount has sat atop a knoll at 411 Main Street since 1804, earning its status as one of Burlington's oldest buildings. It was erected on land that once belonged to Ira Allen. Allen claimed that when he was imprisoned

Grasse Mount, the 1804 residence, much as it looked then, with the later solarium added on the west side. *Courtesy of the author.*

in Europe, the strong-minded attorney and entrepreneur Thaddeus Tuttle and Silas "Baron" Hathaway from St. Albans swindled him out of this and other property. When all was said and done, Tuttle and subsequent owners accumulated a sizable lot of eighty acres on the hill surrounding the house, bounded by Main, South Prospect and South Willard Streets, extending south into the present Overlake neighborhood. Tuttle hired prominent local designer John Johnson, an engineer and surveyor, and Abram Stevens, a carpenter, to design and build his home. Some historians speculate that the original idea for the building may have come from a pattern book template portrayed in the *Winterthur Portfolio*. Wide panoramic views of the lake and mountains awarded this house premier status at the time.

Thaddeus Tuttle was a colorful character with a reputation for going above and beyond in his work and play. According to historian William S. Rann, at one time early in his career, Tuttle was asked by an associate what percentage profit he charged on his goods. After Tuttle replied that he charged 1 percent, the associate denied him credit, saying Tuttle couldn't possibly make a profit and stay solvent with such a low rate. Tuttle recapitulated that he bought his goods for one dollar and then sold them for two dollars, after which he was given credit.

Tuttle's Main Street mansion includes lofty ceilings, a curly maple spiral main staircase with a nautilus-shaped railing and the main entrance on Main Street. Tuttle also owned property in Westford and on Shelburne Point. But his reach exceeded his grasp; eventually, he succumbed to credit problems that saddled so many early property speculators. Unfortunately, by 1824, Tuttle found himself in a world of debt and sold the home on Main Street to Cornelius Van Ness, the eighth governor of Vermont. As we shall see, the noble mansion would have many lives. If only the walls could talk.

On June 29, 1825, French general Marquis de Lafayette visited Burlington. Lafayette, who had fought in the American Revolution and helped America win the war, was on his victory tour of twenty-four states throughout the new country. At 3:00 p.m. on that day, cannons fired on College Street and the two churches on Pearl Street tolled their bells announcing his arrival. General Lafayette and Governor Van Ness arrived in a carriage pulled by four gray horses and a cavalry escort. Thousands greeted the sixty-eight-year old French hero on the UVM green. They paused for a brief welcome ceremony. Lafayette then laid the cornerstone of the Old Mill Building, which was replacing the main UVM college building that had recently burned.

The entourage continued and turned right onto Prospect Street, then left onto Pearl Street, rolling down the hill to Battery Street and then south along the waterfront. It turned left up Main Street and stopped at Governor Van Ness's tavern, at the corner of Main and St. Paul. Lafayette freshened up and then entertained a group of older Revolutionary War veterans. The party moved up to the Grasse Mount mansion for a reception with drinks and snacks from 8:00 p.m. to 11:00 p.m. Lafayette then headed down to the wharf and boarded the steamboat *Phoenix* for Whitehall, New York, then down through the canal after his whirlwind tour of Burlington.

After his term as governor, Van Ness served as the ambassador to Spain for ten years. In his absence, Heman Allen, the nephew of Ira Allen, and his wife rented the mansion. Heman's wife, Elizabeth, loved the mansion and named it Grasse Mount, after the French admiral François Joseph Paul de Grasse, a close friend of Lafayette and commander of the French fleet at the Battle of the Chesapeake in 1781. Admiral de Grasse was instrumental in helping America win the war. Elizabeth Allen died in the house in 1834.

The next owners were retired sea captain Charles Marvin and his wife, Ellen Blackman. They commissioned hand-painted, three-dimensional-effect trompe l'oeil (trick the eye) artwork by French artisans for the building. These works extensively covered the original walls and took years

Trompe l'oeil detail, three-dimensional watercolor painting example on the walls of Grasse Mount, that took years to complete. *Courtesy of the author.*

to complete. The artwork also included quaint landscape scenes painted in closet-sized arched alcoves. Captain Marvin added the belvedere and also installed imported, elegantly carved white marble fireplace mantel surrounds and added several new buildings, including barns, a gardener's cottage and a cottage for Ellen's mother.

They say beauty is in the eye of the beholder, and the next owners, Lawrence Barnes and his wife, possessed different artistic sensibilities than the Marvins. Barnes was remembered as energetic, cheerful and generous, and his personality is seen in their renovations. They painted over much of the earlier wall art with brightly colored oil-paint stencil designs. They also contributed prismatic chandeliers, ornate window headings, artistic etched red glass around the front entrance and the conservatory addition on the west side, taking advantage of the million-dollar views.

The next owner, Edward Wells, of the Wells Richardson Company, who had built a spectacular Queen Anne–style Victorian mansion next door, sold the building to UVM in 1895 for $12,000, a fraction of its value at that time. UVM used it as a women's dormitory until 1971; many alumni remember it today.

As of late, the building is well maintained and appears much as it did in the late 1800s. Samples of the original watercolor-painted walls, oil stencils and carved woodwork in the mansion are preserved and on display for lucky Alumni Foundation employees and alumni to behold.

16
The French Chateau

As late as the 1860s, the Church Street neighborhood was dominated by wood-frame residential homes interspersed with a few businesses and hotels. The towering 170-foot-tall Unitarian Church belfry offered a wide panorama of downtown, from the hill to the lake. Paved sidewalks and dirt streets made for a livable neighborhood, but over the decades, the houses on Church Street began to be replaced by multistory brick commercial buildings. And by 1893, there were even electric streetcar trolleys to move passengers around town and to neighboring towns to the north. Around that time, the white, gambrel-roofed building in the center foreground of the accompanying image, on the corner of Pearl and Church Streets, was demolished. The spectacular Richardson Building was erected in its place.

The Richardson Building was designed by Albany architect Walter Dickson and built in 1895 by Albert E. Richardson and W.B. McKillip. It anchors the east side of the head of Church Street and is counterbalanced by the Masonic Temple, another imposing brick building constructed a few years later on the west side of the street. Richardson intended for his four-and-a-half-story building to provide commercial space on the first two floors and apartment dwellings in the upper stories. Readers may wonder about the source of Richardson's fortune. It turns out that lumber, marble and textiles weren't the only products in demand. In Richardson's case, it was all about selling better living through chemistry.

Church Street in 1860 from the Unitarian Church belfry at the top of Church Street. This panoramic view spans from the hill section on the left to Shelburne Bay on the right. *Unknown photographer, Silver Special Collections, UVM.*

The Richardson Building at the head of Church Street as seen today, relatively unchanged from 1895 when it was built. *Courtesy of the author.*

During the 1870s, four young men—Albert Richardson, William Van Patten, Edward Wells and, later, his brother William—teamed up to form a company named Wells Richardson based in Waterbury, Vermont. They found success marketing and selling innovative chemical dyes and an assortment of patent medicines for various ailments, and moving to Burlington was just the prescription they needed to go big time. Their offices on College Street and, later, St. Paul Street, employed writers, designers, printers, chemists and production staff working in labs and production lines. The company stayed ahead of the curve in the mail-order business, particularly with their wonder drugs.

One popular product in their line of proprietary medicines was called Kidney Wort, purported to be effective for many ailments, including kidney and liver diseases, "feminine problems," piles (hemorrhoids), gravel (kidney stones) and constipation. Another medicine, Paine's Celery, was supposed to cure nervous prostration (mental and physical exhaustion), headaches, neuralgia, weakness and stomach, kidney and liver diseases. These products would be seen as miracle drugs even today. One of the company's marketing tactics was to concoct compelling testimonials from local celebrities to extoll their products' effectiveness. To that end, Bishop Stephen Michaud appeared in the *Burlington Free Press* promoting Paine's Celery. The celebrity endorsement campaign was replicated very successfully in other cities as well; apparently, their products went viral.

Wells Richardson was wildly profitable by the 1880s, and its success lasted for decades. The company partners spent their earnings on lavish mansions and acreage, among other things. But, as with so many things in life, if it sounds too good to be true, it probably is. Their phenomenal success didn't last forever. When the FDA investigated the ingredients in Paine's Celery in the early 1900s, it was found to contain over 20 percent alcohol and amounts of coca, the source of cocaine. Although the medicines may have been popular, the FDA concluded that the feel-good concoctions cured nothing, and they were banned. But that wasn't before the products made the owners a fortune.

Albert Richardson's Church Street building is basically a rectangular, five-by-five-bay brick structure, but the round towers with finials on the west façade lend a blend of French chateauesque and Scottish baronial revival style. The eye-catching appearance of the building adds to the allure of downtown, to say the least. The double-hung windows with brick lintels and architectural detail and the balconies with iron *R*s capped off an elegant appearance on the outside. There was even an elevator inside.

The Heman W. Allen & Company dry-goods store occupied the first and second stories until it was taken over by Allen's partner, Frank Abernethy. Over time, it evolved into Abernethy's Department Store. In a show of family pride, Abernethy's replaced the *R*s on the balconies with *A*s.

In 1919, Abernethy's purchased the adjacent property at 10 Church Street and expanded into the building in 1929, which became Abernethy's Men's Shop. Several decades of successful business followed, which many Vermonters of a certain age today will fondly remember. Residential and office tenants rented spaces on the higher floors. The Richardson Block was the anchor of a vibrant downtown Church Street marketplace. But as the retail landscape evolved in the late 1970s and early '80s with the construction of the University Mall in nearby South Burlington, Abernethy's found its bottom line shrinking. It finally went out of business in 1982. A subsequent owner brought the building up to code and honored the original owner by restoring the iron *R*s on the balconies overlooking Church Street, as originally found on the building.

We don't know what prompted Richardson to build the iconic edifice in 1895. Perhaps he had been inspired by one of his business partners, Edward Wells. In 1891, Wells had built a stunning home at 61 Summit Street.

The Queen Anne Victorian Edward Wells House on Summit Street. *Courtesy of the author.*

Although Wells's Queen Anne Victorian mansion of brick and red limestone doesn't receive the devotion of a full chapter in this book, it still makes the A list and is worthy of mention. The house was designed by Edgar Allan Poe Newcomb of Boston and reveals new craftsmanship details with every glance, such as carved seashell molds that adorn painted short columns, remarkable curved glass and stained-glass windows in round turrets, grandiose woodwork, fireplaces and interior wood carvings completed by master woodworker Albert H. Whittekind. Whittekind left his distinctive work in many old buildings in Burlington, New York City and other cities. The building may look familiar to some readers for another reason.

UVM alumni of certain eras may recall the mansion serving as the home of the Delta Psi fraternity (since 1924). Dr. John Dewey is even included in the ranks of notable Delta Psi alumni. Not to mention the UVM fraternity's high-profile social functions throughout the twentieth century. But after years of declining membership at Delta Psi, some unfortunate transgressions by the fraternity brothers and the building falling into disrepair, the Wells House was acquired by UVM. Today, it serves as a home for the UVM Foundation and alumni functions and is a refreshing reminder of a different time.

17
The Greek Temple

Timothy Follett, who lost his father at the age of ten, graduated with the UVM class of 1810 along with sixteen classmates. Follett quickly became a lawyer and found prominence as the state's attorney, Chittenden County judge and legislator. He also continued with his private enterprises. In 1818, with business partner John Bradley, he built the stone store that stands today on the northwest corner of Maple and Battery Streets, and they owned the Merchants Boat Lake Line canal boat enterprise. The stone store was expanded to its present size in 1827 and sold all kinds of food and commercial products. According to William S. Rann, Follett developed a pulmonary condition that forced some lifestyle adjustments, including a career change. But Follett didn't exactly curb his ambition or work activities.

Follett backed off on his public sector work and threw himself into several new enterprises anchored to shipping and merchandising on Burlington Bay, construction and legal work. By 1840, Follett had become a successful entrepreneur, businessman, developer, and railroad man.

Ammi B. Young, the renowned Vermont Statehouse architect, designed the Follett House, which was built on College Street in 1840 on the north end of a large city block and on a gentle hillside rising from Battery Street. Follett's two-and-a-half-story brick home has a classic Greek Revival structure with a gabled roof, a clapboard exterior and a stone foundation.

Above: The Timothy Follett House on College and Battery Streets. The original main entrance is on the left side of the picture on the College Street wall. *Courtesy of the author.*

Left: The Follett family children, including George, Lorraine, Charles, Lewis and Fred, as noted on the back of the photograph. *Unknown photographer. Silver Special Collections, UVM.*

The main façade gable pediment is supported by five fluted Doric columns. Tall ground-floor windows face the lake on the west elevation, and the second-floor balcony stretches across its width under the pediment. The main entrance is on the north side, on College Street, and is sheltered by a portico. The roof is adorned by a square cupola added in the 1880s. Although at the time the local *Burlington Free Press* noted it was not painted white while Follett lived there, it stood above a beautiful rolling lawn, bridle paths and gardens and claimed magnificent views of the lake and distant high peaks.

Follett and his wife raised their family and entertained guests in their home. Follett and Bradley cofounded and built the Merchants Bank in 1849, the year the railroads came to Burlington. In 1850, the fifty-six-year-old Follett was living with his wife, Lorraine, and five children, aged eighteen to twenty-six in the mansion. Life was good, and business was booming. The family employed three Irish American servants. The extensive grounds covered an entire rectangular city block bordered by Battery, South Champlain, College and Main Streets. But Follett's fortune eventually took a sharp downhill turn.

He had invested most of his assets in the Rutland & Burlington Railroad and had become president of the company. Its main competitor, the Vermont Central Railroad (VCR), which was ambitiously building railways in Vermont, too, got the jump on Follett's company when it beat the Rutland & Burlington to building the northbound rails that would move freight and passengers on new routes to the north to Canada and west to Rouses Point. The Rutland & Burlington (later the Rutland Railroad) crashed. Like so many other successful businessmen who overextended or narrowed their investments during a boom, Follett lost most of his fortune.

Sadly, in 1854, the Follett house was purchased by Follett's industry rival, Henry R. Campbell, who happened to be the superintendent of the rival VCR, which, incidentally, would become Central Vermont Railway in 1872. Follett died in 1857. After the Civil War, the house was sold to an industrialist by the name of Benjamin Nichols. He ran commercial businesses on the waterfront, lived in the house briefly and then sold it and moved to California.

For over a century after that, the building was owned and used by a variety of community organizations, including missions for sick children, housing for women and servicemen, social clubs, church organizations and the Veterans of Foreign Wars. The building survived the controversial urban renewal demolition of the 1960s and a fire that gutted the top floor. It was eventually rescued, acquired and refurbished by local real estate developers Ernest and Antonio Pomerleau. The Follett House is the last of several waterfront mansions that once faced the lake on Battery Street. It stands in plain sight today as a reminder of the success of the work ethic during the shipping era, of architectural beauty and of generous stewardship of historical treasures.

18

The Shining Golden Dome

The birth of the University of Vermont was slow and humble. UVM, chartered in 1791, was one of the first five universities in New England. However, the first president, Reverend Daniel C. Sanders, wasn't hired until 1800. President Sanders served as the sole faculty member for the first graduating class of four students in 1804. The original building, known simply as the "College Building," was constructed on the present site of the Old Mill, overlooking the center of the university green, in 1802.

Designed by the well-known John Johnson of Burlington, the original building contained a two-story chapel, library, museum, medical hall, chemical laboratory, recitation rooms and forty-six student dormitory rooms, which would take years to fill. By 1812, UVM enrolled eighty students and employed five instructors in mathematics, philosophy, astronomy, Greek, Latin, natural history, jurisprudence, medicine, anatomy, surgery and chemistry. But international events interfered with the smooth sailing of the new college. By 1813, Burlington's residents were overrun with thousands of infantrymen and sailors preparing to do battle with the British army and navy. In that year, the college building became a military armory location staffed by soldiers.

The mix of students and soldiers in the College Building during 1813 did not turn out to be a fruitful experience. The storage of arms in the building, soldiers' roughhousing and complaints of pilfering from rooms soon popped the academic bubble. In March 1814, the army requested

Sketch of the original 1802 College Building at UVM by John Johnson. The structure was longer than the sketch indicates. After the 1824 fire, the building was rebuilt with three sections: north, south and middle buildings. *Silver Special Collections, UVM.*

and received a lease to completely take over the hall. Thaddeus Stevens, later a U.S. congressman and prominent figure during the Civil War and Reconstruction, was one of the dozens of students who were sent away for a year until March 1815.

During that school recess, the rooms were used for barracks to house soldiers. On September 11, 1814, during the Battle of Plattsburgh across the lake, people reportedly climbed up into the belfry to try to see the lake and land battles they could hear booming in the distance a few miles north. After the war, students returned, and each year, the enrollment continued to grow. The great hall with its shining golden dome stood as the sole academic building of the university until it was destroyed by fire in 1824.

The following year, UVM began construction of a similar new building designed to be more fire-resistant. It was laid out in three sections, with north (North College) and south (South College) buildings erected first. On June 29, 1825, the cornerstone for the South College building was ceremoniously laid by the visiting Marquis de Lafayette.

In 1829, the Federal-style brick Middle College was built between the north and south buildings, with eight-foot firebreaks between the three buildings. Middle College included the new two-story university chapel on the second and third floors, lecture and recitation rooms, a library, a museum and other facilities, in concert with the design of the first college building.

In 1846, the North, Middle and South Colleges were joined together with parapeted firewalls, creating the state's largest building. Some believed the edifice resembled river mills of the time—it was referred to as "The Mill." Over time, the building became known as the Old Mill.

In 1882, a renovation funded by Burlington native John Purple Howard based on plans by J.J. Randall of Rutland extensively renovated the building in the Victorian Gothic style. This work added a floor with dormers, increased the number of dorm rooms to sixty and replaced the front and side exterior façades and the shining gold dome with the current 150-foot-tall steeple tower, which met mixed reviews. The new tower, which serves as the iconic UVM logo today, was decried and derisively labeled "the birdcage" for several decades. Most of all, the vocal critics wanted the shiny golden dome back.

The renovation created dormitory suites in the north and south wings of the upper floors, heated by cast-iron wood stoves. Colorful wallpapers covered the plaster walls and ceilings. Installing wood stoves in college dorm rooms today would pose an unthinkable risk. However, the next fire wouldn't come from humans but from the heavens above. Lightning struck the South

Left: The Old Mill as it appears today, with the iconic 1882-era steeple, on the site of the original UVM College Building. *Courtesy of the author.*

Opposite: Williams Hall, which sits next to Old Mill on the college green. *Courtesy of the author.*

College end of the Old Mill in 1918, and the ensuing flames destroyed part of the fourth floor and roof before it was miraculously extinguished. Displaced students were moved into dormitory rooms in the newly completed gray stone Converse Hall near the Mary Fletcher Hospital.

In 1968, the chapel on the second floor of the middle building, which might be the most impressive room inside the Old Mill, was rededicated as the John Dewey Memorial Lounge. The lounge includes four two-story arched Tiffany stained-glass windows beneath the high ceiling. The windows honor faculty members George Benedict, James Marsh, Joseph Torrey and John Goodrich and were completed by artisans in 1917. The lounge is an impressive space for study, seminars, events and meetings today.

Williams Hall is another historic and handsome building with a similar scale that sits right next to and north of the Old Mill. The three-and-a-half-story hall was known as Williams Science Hall in 1896, when it was designed and built to provide space for the sciences. The hall boasted state-of-the-art laboratories and even a dynamo to produce electricity for the electrical engineering labs in the building.

Many visitors marvel at the majestic Romanesque entrance arch with terra-cotta medallions overhead that celebrate three outstanding American

scholars at the turn of the nineteenth century: Louis Agassiz (natural history), Samuel F.B. Morse (painter and inventor) and Joseph Henry (electromagnetism). Their likenesses are not to be outdone by the gargoyles that defend the bases of the gabled parapets.

The Old Mill and Williams Hall are just two of several buildings, including the Ira Allen Chapel, the Royall Tyler Theater and Morrill Hall, that face the green on University Place. Each one stands as an attractive structure, and together they own enough history for another volume. But there is one more building on the green that is particularly captivating.

19
UVM's Jewel

UVM's awe-inspiring Billings Library has been described as the university's architectural gem and is located on University Place, north of the Old Mill and next to Williams Hall. Woodstock, Vermont native Frederick Billings funded the building to create and house the extensive library of twelve thousand volumes of another Woodstock native, George Perkins Marsh. Marsh was a prominent conservationist, congressman and diplomat, as well as a remarkable philologist. He spoke and wrote in over twenty languages and had recently passed away in 1882, when Billings started the library project.

Frederick Billings was a noted lawyer and retired president of the Northern Pacific Railroad and namesake of Billings, Montana, where the railroad established the town as a trade hub. Billings had high aspirations and had been disappointed in his initial attempts to find an architectural design that he liked.

Ultimately, Billings settled on a design by Henry Hobson Richardson, one of the country's most influential architects of the era. Richardson also designed the State Capitol in Albany, New York; Trinity Church in Boston; Allegheny County Courthouse in Pittsburgh; and Sever Hall at Harvard University. The Richardsonian Romanesque style of architecture in Billings includes its imposing reddish-brown sandstone exterior with beautiful carvings, the classic arched entrance, the black slate roof with "eye-brow" dormers and the round stone towers. The design and construction of the library took place from 1883 to 1885.

Billings Memorial Library, southwest elevation, as it looked when it was built in 1885. *Courtesy of the author.*

The main façade of the library looks westward over the University Green. A large front-gabled pavilion is flanked by towers joined by a wide Syrian arch to shelter the entrance under a small porch. Five arched-top windows look out through an arcade, with three narrow lancet windows above them. A small round seal anchors the gable peak. The octagonal tower on the left rises above the building with an open belfry. The right tower is round and much shorter. A long, low wing with a band of windows and a hipped roof stretches to the left with squat towers at both corners. More windows encircle the polygonal room on the right side.

Many current Vermont Catamounts and alumni know why this special place has been a prime student study space for over a century. The library interior is at least as inspiring as the outside. The spacious front entrance hall Reading Room features a central medieval-style oak fireplace, a towering open timber cathedral ceiling and a large oil portrait of Frederick Billings over the fireplace. A deep, rectangular, two-story wing with an open timber ceiling sits to the left of the entrance. To the right, a full-height wood-and-plaster archway leads to the apse, with a full balcony and a second story of alcoved shelving for the Marsh Collection. The ceiling is supported with

The apse polygonal south room inside Billings Memorial Library. *Courtesy of the author.*

hammerbeam trusses and rich foliate carving that exudes an awesome character and ambiance.

The original cost of the library was expected to be $75,000, but Billings paid $150,000 by the time it was completed. The final tab included scaling back some of the original materials and details in the craftsmanship. Henry Richardson died the year after the library was completed in 1885. Many of the original gas lighting fixtures have remained, although the building was electrified in 1911.

Several additions expanded the space due to the ever-growing volumes and student enrollment. In 1889, the north room was extended twenty-five feet to accommodate more stacks, and a forty-by-forty-foot Marsh Room was added to the east, behind the central fireplace in the entry.

Major expansions came in the twentieth century, with two big construction additions. First, in the 1960s, a large new library was built on Main Campus. Twenty years later, a student center was added onto the back and beneath Billings Library. This created additional room for a theater, classrooms and dining space that doesn't impact the integrity of the original architectural gem.

V

UNCOMMON GROUNDS

20

The Military Base

In 1813, Sylvester Churchill of the Third U.S. Artillery, formerly of Woodstock, Vermont, supervised the building of a thirteen-cannon emplacement on the edge of the bluff overlooking Burlington Bay in what is now Battery Park. The fortification, known as Churchill's Battery, was built of sand and sod blocks taken from the surrounding lots. On August 2, a raiding party including two British ships and a row galley pulled into Burlington Bay, dropped anchors and fired their cannons at the fortifications and some of the buildings in Burlington for about twenty minutes. At least two cannonballs hit buildings, and a few balls have been recovered from the bluff below what is today's Battery Park.

One building that was hit is still standing at the southwest corner of Pine and Main Streets. At the time, that building was the residence of Commodore Thomas MacDonough, the commander of the U.S. Navy fleet on Lake Champlain. His fleet was being outfitted and prepared in Burlington for the impending battle with the British fleet in what would be remembered as the Battle of Plattsburgh. Fortunately, in 1813, a couple of MacDonough's ships sat in the bay near the Maple Street wharf, each armed with a twelve-pound cannon. The military cantonment, or base, where Battery Park is today, was protected by fortifications and cannons that returned fire on the British ships. The exchange resulted in no American casualties.

Burlington, which had two thousand citizens at the time, was a focal point of that war, with up to four thousand enlisted men staying at the military base at one time. Most of the American officers roomed in boardinghouses and hotels; the enlisted men stayed in tents or barracks during the three-year

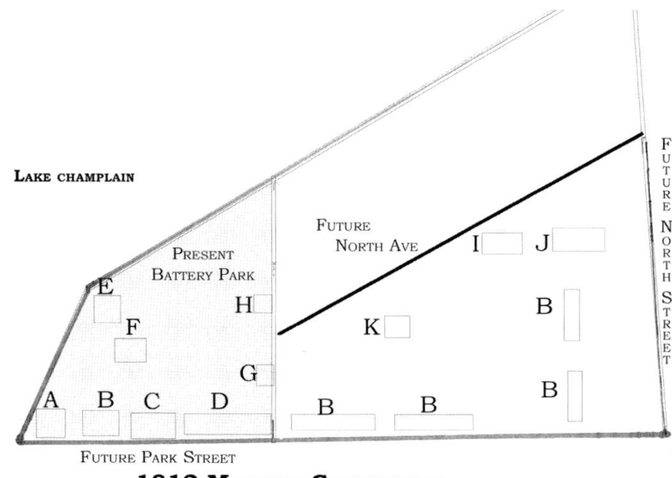

The 1812 military base sketch, including the present-day Battery Park (shaded area). The letters indicate several long barracks (B), a powder magazine (G), a guard sentry house (A), officers' quarters (C), a gun shed (I), an armory (F), stables (J), storehouses (H, K), the battery (E) and a hospital (D). *Courtesy of the author.*

War of 1812. On September 11, 1814, after a bloody battle, MacDonough was victorious, defeating the British fleet in the Battle of Plattsburgh, ending British rule of the lake for good.

Today's Battery Park land was then privately owned, and the forest had been cleared in June 1812 by the men of the Eleventh U.S. Infantry, led by Revolutionary War hero Colonel Isaac Clark. Eventually, the garrison built winter quarters with fourteen buildings that included the following, shown on the accompanying map: several long barracks, a powder magazine, a guard sentry house, officers' quarters, a gun shed, an armory, stables, storehouses, the battery and a hospital.

During those few years, the population of Burlington was dwarfed by the Eleventh Cavalry and an additional thirty regiments from New Hampshire, Maine, Massachusetts, Connecticut, New York and at least seven other states. The ballooning military presence spawned booming economic opportunities for a few years. Among the opportunists were the Mayo brothers from Orwell, who opened two bakeries on nearby Maple Street and secured a government contract to supply bread to the navy fleet.

Margaret Chandonette, a French American, ran a successful tavern in a white, two-story frame house with a gambrel roof on the northeast corner of Battery and Main Streets. Apparently, Chandonette's tavern was popular with soldiers and camp followers for drinking and carousing in their spare time. Other tavern owners, tailors, bootmakers, blacksmiths, booksellers and coopers benefited from the temporary population boom.

But not everyone was impressed with the military presence. In 1813, a merchant named John Parker Wiswall had moved his family into a house on the southwest corner of Battery and College Streets. Wiswall, who had strong British Loyalist inclinations, was clearly not a fan of the garrison. Apparently, he butted heads with some of the soldiers and was outspoken about his political sentiments. At one point, when several soldiers confronted him at his house, the conversation escalated at gunpoint. As they say, a man's home is his castle, and Wiswall must have felt endangered. During the altercation, he shot and killed one of the soldiers. The soldiers returned the following night and burned his house down. He and his family fled to Cambridge, Vermont, then back to New York not long after.

In another account, several armed soldiers liberated several of their buddies from the town jail on Church Street after they had been incarcerated for theft. The town residents were overrun by the military. As previously mentioned, the soldier presence in the College Building at UVM was too close for comfort. In March 1814, the army leased the building and the students were released for a year, except for the medical students, who stayed with their professor, Dr. Pomeroy, at his house (which still stands) at 166 Battery Street. Pomeroy actually served as a surgeon in the base hospital. His adult son, also a medical doctor, died in a flu epidemic during the war, and diseases were prevalent at the time.

Typhoid, measles and dysentery were common, and influenza (pneumonia) was a rampant epidemic in Burlington during those years. The hospital also treated hundreds of battle-injured patients from Chateaugay and Lacolle Mills, both in Quebec, and from Plattsburgh. The two-story hospital building at the military base measured twenty by three hundred feet and was staffed by surgeons, surgeon's mates, apothecaries, cooks, guards and ward masters. The hospital's capacity was 300 patients, but at one time in 1814, the hospital needed to use barracks and other buildings to treat a total of 900 patients. Military records show that 550 soldiers died at the hospital during the war.

One account of medical treatment, chronicled by Dr. Thomas Mann, a surgeon on Crab Island during the Battle of Plattsburgh and later at the Burlington military hospital, is not for the faint of heart. Not only gruesome battle injuries, but epidemics such as influenza savagely attacked soldiers and civilians, and the casualties were significant. After the Battle of Plattsburgh, hundreds of men who had been treated at Crab Island during the battle on the lake were moved in boats to Burlington to convalesce. Best practices in medicine at the time included treatments such as blistering, purging, bloodletting, calomel (mercury), lead apatite and alcohol. Amputations were not aseptic by any means, and infections were common. Germs had not been discovered yet.

However, Dr. Mann was an innovator in his time. In his journal, Dr. Mann speculated that close quarters in tents and stagnant indoor spaces seemed to spread diseases and infections. He recommended separating patients and air ventilation as much as possible. Alcohol was used as a cure-all, and as we know today, it usually did more harm than good. The high number of deaths left behind a hallowed legacy that is largely hidden near the base.

At least two dozen 1812-era corpses have been unearthed north of the present Battery Park property, in the vicinity of nearby North Street and present-day North Avenue. Many of the bodies were clad in long shirts or sheets; some were dressed in shirts and trousers. Some showed signs of trauma or injury, while others had died of disease. All were buried in hexagonal wood coffins.

After the war, one building was leased to the town to be used as a poorhouse. Some of the remaining buildings were offered for sale, and some were looted for materials. In the 1820s, the Champlain Glass Company occupied some of the buildings, and tenement housing was built along the edge of the lake. Part of the hospital remained on site as late as 1838. Eventually, several private owners of the present Battery Park lots donated their land to the city of Burlington. Churchill's Battery was completely leveled in 1938. The WPA built a low stone wall at the western edge of the park overlooking the bay and mountains. Today, Battery Park is a public space for memorials, gatherings, concerts and recreation.

21

The Ledges

In 1850, a man named Napoleon Proctor built a shipyard in today's South Cove, which was then known as Mark's Bay. Shelburne Point sheltered the cove from prevailing southwesterly winds, making it ideal for building commercial ships. The South Cove shipyard prospered in the late 1800s and into the early 1900s. The magnificent location caught the eye of Dr. William Seward Webb, a Columbia University–educated physician and later Wall Street investor, railroad tycoon and future Vermont state congressman. Webb and his family lived in a Fifth Avenue mansion. He enjoyed financial success and expensive hobbies.

In 1874, the twenty-three-year-old Dr. Webb, who kept his yacht in the cove, bought 245 acres north of South Cove. In 1883, Dr. Webb and his wife, Lila, built a "summer cottage" near the lake. Most people would call the cottage a mansion, and it included a compound with fine horse stables, barns and other outbuildings. He called his property Oakledge. The Webb family cottage sat where the picnic shelter is today, a couple hundred feet from the water. Webb's son J. Watson Webb was born at Oakledge in 1884, grew up and went on to marry Electra Havemeyer. They would become the founders of the Shelburne Museum.

Dr. Webb used his considerable assets and good taste to landscape the spectacular gentleman's farm property with winding, rocky bridle paths and manicured gardens. But before long, Webb found a property he liked better near Shelburne Point. Or, we should say, he found a number of properties. In all, he bought thirty-two contiguous farms. By 1885, he had consolidated them into a charming grand estate and moved his horses and yachts there, at the present location of Shelburne Farms, where his endeavors prospered on almost four thousand aces overlooking the lake.

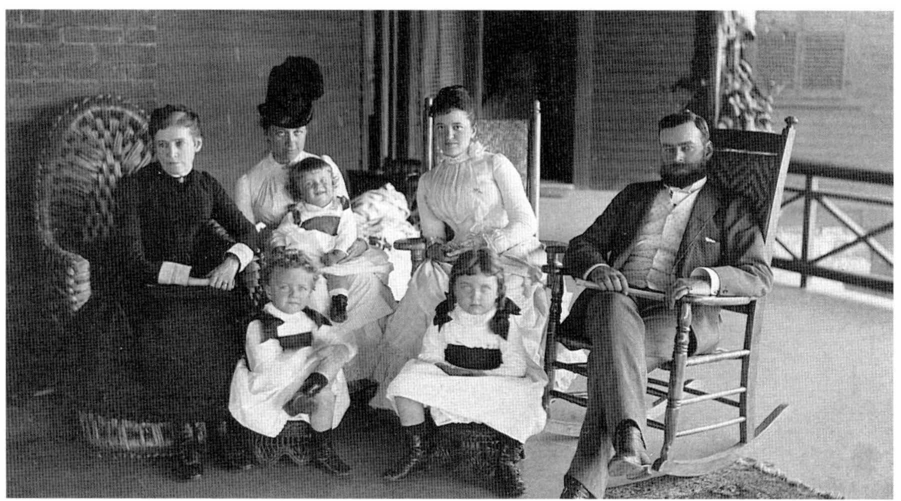

The Webb family. *From front left*: children Frederica and James; *back row*: Laura, Mrs. Walter Webb holding Walter Webb Jr., Lila Osgood Webb and Dr. William Seward Webb. *Shelburne Farms Collection, Shelburne, Vermont.*

In 1891, Dr. Webb commissioned a survey of the Oakledge property, which sat adjacent to the nearby railroad tracks. The land was subdivided into more than two hundred lots. Fortunately, the subdivision and sale were never accomplished. Webb eventually passed the property on to his daughter, Fredrica Webb Jones, who would use the property as her own summer home.

In 1925, Jones sold the property to a group of Burlington businessmen. They added a cluster of summer cottages for their personal use. The property remained largely underused until 1929. At that time, the mansion became part of the Oakledge Manor Resort, which was run by Allen P. Beach of Basin Harbor Club, the popular lakeside resort in Ferrisburgh. Fred C. Hill purchased and managed the resort from 1934 until 1953, when he leased it to Beach's son David. According to Basin Harbor host Bob Beach Jr., after eight years of leasing, the Beach family bought the property and immediately sold it to a group of General Electric employees in 1961.

The employees rebranded the resort into the Cliffside Country Club and enjoyed it as a private club. In 1970, the Burlington Parks Department purchased the 45-acre club for $230,000 and later bought an additional 320 acres of surrounding property. Later that year (historians, please avert your eyes), the cottage was burned to ashes by the Burlington Fire Department in a training exercise. The remaining barns and stables were demolished, erasing most of the evidence of the original historic Webb estate forever, except for a few foundations and chimneys. Since then, Oakledge has served as a year-round public park alongside residential and commercial developments.

22

Down by the River

The mouth of the Winooski River at the junction of Lake Champlain has been a high-traffic area for thousands of years, especially when water was the chief mode of transportation. But one era of recorded history at the mouth of the river stands out, although it is all but forgotten and hidden from today's view.

It all started with a man named John S. Derway, who had bought the Bigelow Farm at the mouth of the Winooski River in 1865. Derway eventually set aside part of the farm as a park. He named it Riverside Park and built a small hotel. His son John L. Derway built a wildly successful seasonal clambake business that beckoned the masses from cities such as Boston and New York to dine, fish and vacation at his Riverside Park House. His newspaper ads promised unsurpassed fishing and first-class fish dinners. Apparently, Derway was able to deliver on his promises. Comments in the *Burlington Free Press* in the late 1800s confirm that the Riverside was booming and more popular than ever.

In 1895, Derway Sr. sold the resort to William Chambers and his wife, Lizzie. The two expanded the hotel and amenities on the site. Local couples trekked by land and water, twenty-five to thirty at a time, for dinner and dancing on Saturday nights. Others came to stay for weeks at a time at the hotel: some were local, and some hailed from out of state. As time marched on, all kinds of exciting adventures began to unfold at the hotel site. At the end of the 1890s, the northward railroad construction began. That meant large crews of construction workers moving into the area and working for months. The railroad crew built a big shanty nearby for their base of operations. After their hard labors, construction workers became thirsty and tapped into the ready supply of alcohol at the hotel lounge.

At its peak, the hotel boasted nine rooms and a bathroom upstairs and five rooms downstairs, heated with stoves. There were dining facilities, hot and cold water, ingrain (reversible) carpets, double windows, screens, curtains, an icehouse, a barn, a covered buggy, a heavy express wagon and seven boats. The failing health of Mr. Chambers forced him to sell the hotel in 1904. In that year, they offered the package for $5,000 or best offer. The hotel property would change hands several times in the next couple of decades.

One Riverside Hotel owner, a man by the name of Jack Powers, was notable. On one occasion, he served drinks in the morning to several railroad workers who had decided to take a break from their hard labor moving earth and laying tracks. Once the railroad workers were loosened up a bit, how could they not resist trying their luck at hooking the big one, right there at the unsurpassed fishing mecca? After they commandeered a hotel boat without permission, Mr. Powers confronted the fishermen. A language barrier and explosive tempers didn't improve communication, and an altercation between the workers and Powers ensued. The conversation turned physical, and somebody whacked Powers on the back of the head with an oar. After exchanging further niceties, Powers retreated inside to cool off. But that wasn't the end of it.

His wife almost immediately called to him to come to the door. There he found several of the men, armed with rocks, sticks and cans, calling him outside to settle things like a man. Powers pulled down his trusty loaded shotgun and headed out the door with the intention of ordering them off his property once and for all.

In the scuffle that ensued, one barrel of the gun discharged, Powers was wounded in a couple of places, and it is safe to say that nobody got what they wanted. Powers was sent to Mary Fletcher Hospital. Burlington's finest police were called and a couple of the workers were charged. Fortunately for all involved, Powers survived. But that wasn't the only dramatic episode at the hotel. The legend of the mouth of the river grew with the presence of the Rutland Railroad.

After 1900, the railroad tracks ran by the hotel property and included a double bridge over the Winooski River, within eyesight of the hotel. In 1908, a young man's body was found floating twenty feet from the hotel. His wristwatch had stopped at 8:25, presumably the time of impact. An investigation found no evidence of foul play. It was believed that he had

The Winooski River railroad bridge. The photo was taken adjacent to the Riverside Park Hotel location. *Courtesy of the author.*

fallen off the bridge. The hotel continued to be fairly popular, especially with sportsmen.

The business changed hands several times and was also rented for a while and began to attract attention in the neighborhood. In 1910, a trio of co-owners was charged with allowing disorderly people to hang out, although cooler heads prevailed and the parties were not charged. Newspaper stories recount a few police raids (common everywhere in that era) uncovering illegal drinking and "immoral activities" with "ladies." Of course, in those days, the names of suspects in both parties were printed for all to see in the local papers.

During Prohibition, the mouth of the river was a popular location for bootleggers and rumrunners, spawning alcohol stills and speakeasies in the neighborhood. After the Flood of 1927, when the bridge was destroyed, bridge reconstruction crews populated the area once again and bought liquor from the locals. Historian David Blow reported legends of crooked deals, "fancy houses," fights over women and bad whiskey at the mouth of the river.

These legendary stories of the area and specifically at the hotel are given credibility by longtime resident and owner of Charlie's Boathouse at the mouth of the river, Christine Auer Hebert. She said there were year-round homes on both sides of the railroad tracks in the neighborhood. According to Hebert, John Derway had demolished many of those homes, and her family enjoyed their own summer cottage on the lake. In an interview, ninety-four-year-old Hebert said, "The story we were told was, men used to go see the ladies at what they called 'The Ladies' House.'" Apparently, the hotel earned a reputation as a house of ill repute, and the locals were not impressed. The hotel mysteriously burned down and was never rebuilt. Hebert confirmed that the location of the hotel sat on the east corner of North Avenue and Cove Road, maybe forty to fifty feet from the corner. It would have easily been accessible by land or by a short canal from the river. Today, that lot is a patch of woods in a neighborhood of year-round homes on either side of Cove Road.

All that is left of the ladies' house today is a depression in the woods. The rail line has been paved and repurposed as the Burlington Greenway for runners, walkers and bikers. The adjacent tiny marina was recently acquired by the countywide Winooski Valley Park District and named Derway Island Park. Today's neighborhood is a quaint, respectable riverside community.

VI

WELCOME TO THE WARDS

23
THE OLD EAST END

In 1772, Green Mountain Boys Ira Allen and Remember Baker built a twenty-by-thirty-two-foot blockhouse with thirty-two-gun ports on the north edge of the river at the present location of the Winooski roundabout. By 1773, Allen had surveyed and bought twenty thousand acres in Burlington and over seventy thousand acres in Vermont, mostly on credit. He and his associates cut a path from the Winooski River to Middlebury, which follows the present path of today's Route 116. Later, they cut another path to the Lake Champlain waterfront, along the high ground that is now known as Colchester Avenue, Pearl Street and Battery Street. On the steeper south bank of the river, the very earliest settlement in Burlington emerged on what the residents called the East End. This settlement was the industrial birthplace of the city, as it supported logging, farming, milling and manufacturing by the late 1780s.

By 1786, there were already two sawmills and a gristmill on the Burlington side of the river, and the biggest concentration of Burlington's residents lived and worked in that neighborhood. Many of the surrounding acreage and buildings were originally owned by Moses and Guy Catlin, George Edgecombe and Ira Allen and his Onion River Land Company. Colchester Avenue and Chase Street were the main arteries, with businesses sprouting up and growing along the river.

Looking at receipts, letters and records from the era reveals a juggernaut of business arrangements that were overwhelmingly based on promissory notes. Land, buildings and businesses, materials, crops and other commodities were often leased, with balloon payments due after a term of months or years. Often, notes were sold or traded to other people, even multiple times. Currency was scarce, so barter and notes were a common way to do business. As we might imagine, this scenario created a lot of debtors when people were not able to pay off the notes. Lawsuits resulted in honest men, even Ira Allen, being sued and trying to avoid going to debtor's jail until their debts were paid.

The accompanying 1795 map shows the layout of the area, which is easily recognizable today. Note that there was a ferry to get across the river above the high falls, early roads and a handful of buildings on either side of the river, including the first mills. Much of the land was devoted to food production, and the first covered bridge connecting Colchester Avenue to Main Street in Colchester (later Winooski) wouldn't be built for almost one hundred years.

Allen ran a trading post, and some believe that the original building still exists at the corner of Colchester Avenue and Barrett Street. Edgecombe's house and tavern, built in 1791 and still standing, sat halfway up the avenue at number 411. By 1795, it was called Ames Tavern, as noted on the map. Across the road from the tavern was a tenement house with a store next door.

The early settler Moses Catlin married Lucinda Allen, Ira Allen's niece. When Catlin sold his first house to the notable Burlington architect and builder John Johnson, the story goes, Lucinda wanted to have the best view in Burlington. Therefore, he bought acreage at the very top of the hill to build the Catlin Farm, which he eventually sold to Mary Fletcher and today is the site of the UVM Medical Center's main campus.

The first businesses centered on logging and milling the obvious resource: old-growth forest wood. Another promising industry was the production of potash, which was in high demand in Canada and England. Timber rafts were convenient but unwieldy and dangerous ways to move logs, milled lumber, potash and other products. The rafts could be outfitted with sails and shanties, would float down the river and hopefully catch a prevailing south wind to blow seventy miles north to St. John on the Richelieu River, and even to Montreal when the river was high enough to override the shoals.

In the 1700s, the men who settled the East End were often prior associates of the Allens and largely transplants from Connecticut and Massachusetts. Many were Revolutionary War veterans and were commonly referred to as Yankees. They tended to be well acquainted with the Protestant faith or didn't formally worship at all. As a group, their heritage was relatively homogeneous. But the population was about to become more diverse.

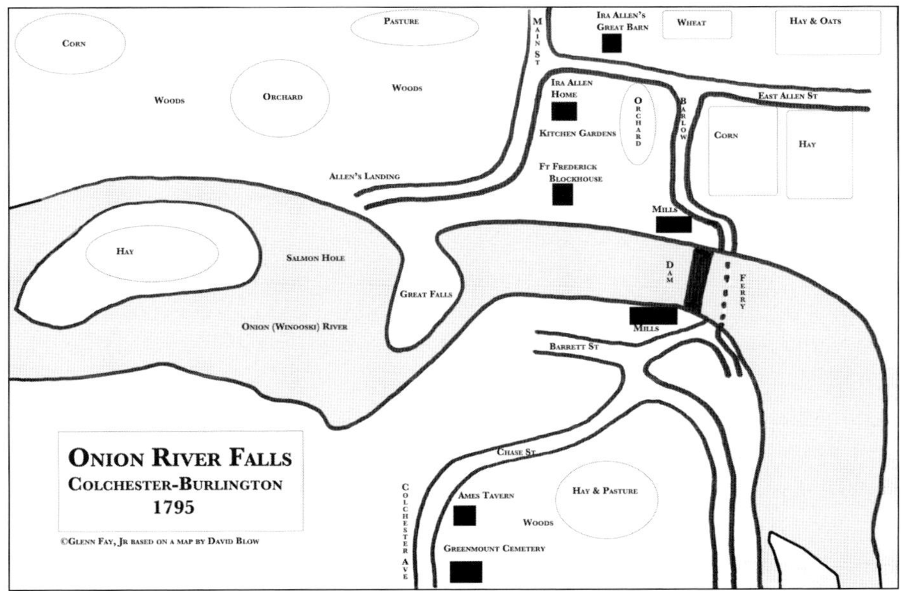

A 1795 Onion River Falls map of the early settlement of Burlington (*south of the river*) and Colchester (*north of the river*). This part of Colchester is now the City of Winooski. *Courtesy of the author.*

The enormous energy of the mighty Onion River attracted woolen mills on both banks at the falls. By the early 1800s, the river powered a clothier works (1802), a fine-yarn mill (1814) and a paper mill, converting cloth rags to paper on the Burlington riverside. All of the mills required labor. As soon as the mills were conceived, a labor force was needed to build and then staff them. By the mid-1800s, the mills required hundreds of workers. With the arrival of French Canadian millworkers, Burlington's ethnicity changed and would steadily evolve with the continual arrival of new workers over the next one hundred years.

A patent block mill for ship rigging was built in 1835, but it burned in 1838. A few years later, cotton and woolen mills were built near the site of the present Chace Mill. By the late 1800s, thousands of millworkers were employed and housed in the East End neighborhood. The labor force was almost exclusively French Canadian, including many children. Photographer Lewis Wickes Hines documented many child laborers working in the mills and in lumbering and woodworking shops between 1909 and 1910 in Burlington and other mill cities. Hines noted that few of the boys spoke English. The job opportunities resulted in immigrants moving in and living in tenements, duplexes and single-family homes that filled in the hillside near the river.

But nature seemed to almost continually be at odds with the medium-term success of the river mills. Letters from Ira Allen to his brother Levi in 1786 tell of severe flooding destroying all of the mills on the river. Everything had to be rebuilt. Devastating floods destroyed some or all of the mills in 1798, 1817, 1828, 1830 and 1927; and fires swept through in 1838, 1852, 1859 and 1891. Most of the mills were eventually sold and rebuilt with improvements by new buyers willing to take a gamble. Today, some of the surviving mill buildings serve as housing and businesses in a quaint, small-scale, urban-chic neighborhood that spans both sides of the river.

24
Burlington Bay

As the early mills rose along the Winooski River on the east side of town, the shallow shoreline of Burlington Bay beckoned lumber shipping. Water Street, now known as Battery Street, became a hub of the early neighborhood along the lake. Many of the first Yankee settlers of the bay area became farmers and entrepreneurs. Early on, it became clear that the bay, located on the great Lake Champlain superhighway, offered enormous potential as a commercial port.

On visiting Burlington, novelist Nathaniel Hawthorne described the cast of diverse characters, including Yankee Green Mountain Boys, Montreal merchants, British officers, country squires, French Canadians, Scotsmen, tourists from the south and swarms of Irish emigrants taking jobs on the Burlington waterfront. And there were plenty of jobs.

The shipping business infrastructure required everything from pick-and-shovel earthworks to logging, construction, shipbuilding and every aspect of a supply chain and new economy that was growing around the bay. Irish and Canadian laborers continuously flocked in to take jobs and earn a living.

In the 1820s and '30s, hundreds of Irish men and women journeyed to Vermont, looking for a life they could only dream of in Ireland. In the Green Mountains, men could own their own land, which wasn't a possibility back on the Emerald Isle. The early Irish laborers came from northern Ireland and entered through Canada, since at that time entry tariffs were charged at American ports. The towns of Fairfield, Underhill, Moretown, Castleton, Middlebury and Burlington experienced what some historians call "chain

Burlington Bay was the third-largest lumber shipping port, behind Chicago and Albany, New York, in the 1870s. Before it was backfilled, the shoreline lay at Water (Battery) Street. *Silver Special Collections, UVM.*

migration." Settlers would move in; find readily available work in logging, farming, mills or service work; and rave to their relatives back home about the abundant opportunities in Vermont. This would lead to more family members joining them in Vermont.

The Irish Potato Famine of 1845–48 fueled an influx of starving and weary Irish people desperate for work, and they constituted 30 percent of the city by the 1850s. The mini–Industrial Revolution and its mills, new railroads and shipping created a booming economy around Burlington Bay. According to a comprehensive research project by Vince Feeney and Brendan Keleher, most of the Irish worked as unskilled laborers. Some of the women worked as teachers or found jobs as domestic servants or in the needle trades.

At that time, the inexpensive rentals available to the poorest arrivals were close to Lake Champlain near Battery Street and on rural North Street. According to Feeney, faced with prejudice, many Irish Americans toiled in the most difficult and lowest-paying occupations, including in the lumber, marble and shipping industries. A coherent Irish community gathered in the Battery Street neighborhood and included Irish-owned boardinghouses and taverns. Neighborhood churches provided community support and networking for newcomers. Irish tavern owners on Battery Street were likely to have the support of their Irish American neighbors.

The preponderance of Irish and French Canadians working on the waterfront, and the lack of African American laborers, raises the question of racism in hiring. The forty male and female African Americans living in Burlington in 1860 were overwhelmingly employed as barbers and in domestic-servant positions.

Another ethnic group, this time from Italy, arrived in Burlington around 1890. They were principally male railroad workers and laborers who built the railroad beds, laid water pipes in the outlying towns and installed railroad tracks between Burlington and elsewhere. Italian work crews exclusively built the Rutland-Canadian Railroad northward through the Champlain Islands. Most of the hundreds of laborers and railroad workers left their wives and families back home in Italy or in other American cities. A makeshift neighborhood was built at the present-day Burlington High School Institute Road location, housing the railroad gangs. A few other Italians worked in the food industry and as fruit sellers in Burlington.

As the century turned, an Italian neighborhood coalesced on the city block bordered by Battery Street to the west of Church Street, in an area known as the urban core. Another migration occurred at the end of the nineteenth century and in the first couple of decades of the twentieth century. People from Italy, Syria, Greece and other countries appeared in the Queen City, looking for work. Many of them lived in the urban core and the North End and found work, advancement and a cohesive community in Burlington.

Over time, the new Americans assimilated into the middle class through the professions and successful business ownership. Italians and French Canadians, who worshipped at Catholic churches such as the Cathedral of the Immaculate Conception and St. Joseph's Church, sometimes intermarried and formed families. Within a few decades, the city would completely transform the Burlington Bay neighborhood into retail and commercial space, and "Little Italy" would become a nostalgic memory. The urban renewal project of the 1960s, described in chapter 27, would replace most of the urban core working-class neighborhoods with a shopping mall, offices and hotels.

Later on in the twentieth century, city leaders began to look at the old industrial infrastructure of the waterfront west of Battery Street and envision change. They saw an area that needed to be cleaned up and redeveloped in an environmentally conscious way. Melinda Moulton and

Elizabeth Steele cofounded the Main Street Landing and implemented a forty-year transformation of the lakefront. The result is a $30 million, 250,000-square-foot, healthy, accessible and affordable center with events, retail and recreational and office space.

25
The North Street Enclaves

During the early 1800s, the Church Street area remained primarily a residential district with homes and large gardens. The waterfront became a commercial and industrial center. North Street, which lay a block north of and parallel to Pearl Street, was still a rural landscape. It was unique, as it would evolve to be the only early commercial artery surrounded by a residential area. Ammi B. Young's 1830 map, which includes symbols for existing building footprints, depicted only a handful of scattered buildings along North Street at that time, visible parallel to the top of the accompanying map.

The improvement of several regional transportation routes spurred accelerated business development. The Champlain Canal connected Burlington to the Hudson River and New York City when it opened in 1823. The long-awaited completion of the Chambly Canal on the Richelieu River in 1843 opened up seamless commerce from Burlington to Montreal and Quebec City, Halifax and beyond. To top it off, by 1849, both the Vermont Central (Central Vermont) and Rutland Railroads had come to town.

With rail transportation, Burlington freight and passengers were connected with markets in New York City, Boston and Montreal, and travel times were cut drastically. By then, lumber, blown glass and textiles were the primary goods produced in the factories of Burlington and neighboring Colchester. Burlington was said to be the third-largest lumber port in the United States, behind Chicago and Albany, New York. Half of the structures throughout the city built between 1860 and 1910 supported the booming lumber and textile industries.

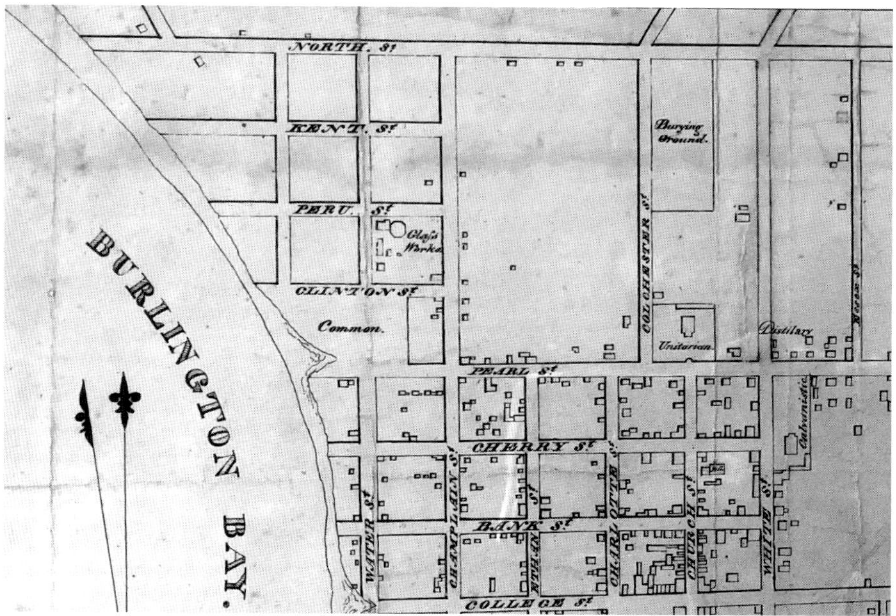

Plan of Burlington Village, 1830, by Ammi B. Young. This, the top left corner of the Young map, shows six buildings marked on North Street at that time. *Silver Special Collections, UVM.*

As labor needs increased and immigrants arrived, the population of Burlington became more diverse. By 1870, one-third of the population was French Canadian, and that community condensed near North Street and Elmwood Avenue, centered around St. Joseph's Church, which had a French-speaking priest. Feeney and Keleher caution that not all Canadian immigrants spoke French. As many as 15 percent of Canadian immigrants were not Francophones; some were originally from Ireland, Scotland and other countries.

During the 1880s until the turn of the century, a number of Lithuanian Jews, who were escaping religious persecution, emigrated from Lithuania to Burlington in large numbers. They settled and built a community in the still-rural area around North Street, especially near the intersections of Hyde, Archibald and Prospect Streets, where the Ohavi Zedek Synagogue was built in 1887.

By the 1890s, a strong Irish neighborhood had emerged close to the waterfront along North Street between North Avenue and North Champlain Street. At about the same time and during the decades that followed, more young French Canadians looking for better opportunities continued to arrive in Burlington to become farmers, lumbermen and laborers in brickyards and textile mills. A few blocks down North Avenue on Crowley Street, a group of German immigrants settled the block near the still-existing Goethe Lodge and formed a small community.

According to Feeney, 50 percent of Burlington's twenty thousand residents were first- or second-generation immigrants by 1910. Those who didn't work in the lumberyards worked in the textile mills, on the wharves, on ships or in businesses in the North Street commercial center. Some of those businesses competed with those on Church Street, which was by then emerging as a shopping center hub.

The various immigrant groups each followed a similar community development process. Newcomers came to Burlington seeking jobs. Religion offered faith, support, common ground and a center for social activities. The North End was the binding agent that gave them community and set the stage for a new life.

Places of worship for most of Burlington's ethnic groups offered schools, choirs, sports leagues, scouting, mothers' clubs, men's clubs, prayer groups and other social organizations. Singing, dancing and feasting were common activities. Most of the ethnic groups initially became more geographically concentrated, but over time, those cultures, including native languages, eventually waned and almost disappeared.

The following dates reflect peak immigration periods: Irish, between 1840 and 1850; French Canadian, between 1865 and 1870; Lithuanian Jews, between 1880 and 1900; and Russian Jews, between 1904 and 1908.

Peak Immigration of Ethnic Groups in Burlington

1800	1820	1840	1860	1880	1900	1910	1920	1940
		Irish						
			French/Canadian					
				Lithuania, Russia, Poland				
					Italy, Syria, Greece			

In contrast to other immigrant groups, very few Jewish women worked as domestic servants; most worked in their own homes. Peddlers who started out in Burlington with a backpack or a vendor cart often succeeded to the point that, within a few years, they had become merchants with their own stores. A department store, a pastry shop, an economy store, grocery stores, tradesmen's shops and other Jewish-operated shops lined North Street. The vibrant businesses and stable residential neighborhood resulted in the community being identified as "Little Jerusalem."

The Jewish emigration from Lithuania, Russia and Poland continued until around 1920. According to historian Jeff Potash, personality squabbles within the community led to the building of three Orthodox places of worship within a city block. The original Ohavi Zedek Synagogue was built in 1885 on Archibald Street; the Chi Adam Synagogue on Hyde Street in 1889; and the Ahavath Gerim Synagogue, nearby, also on Archibald Street, in 1909. Many of the Jews practiced Orthodox religion and preserved the Yiddish language for decades.

Because of the still rural nature of the North End, complemented with barns, livestock and gardens, life in the Jewish community resembled Eastern European shtetl village life. Businesses, movie theaters and the Hebrew Free School became social gathering places. Most Jewish children attended H.O. Wheeler School, a public school on Archibald Street, and almost half of its enrollment was Jewish. Men who lived in the neighborhood remember going to Hebrew school on Winooski Avenue for lessons every day after school from 4:00 to 5:30 p.m.

The new generation was becoming wealthier, allowing them to buy larger houses in other neighborhoods. Intermarriage became more prevalent, and with continual assimilation, by World War II, the North End was no longer the distinct ethnic neighborhood it had been. As the families assimilated into the larger community in the 1920s and '30s, English became increasingly intermingled with Yiddish, and the old traditions slowly eroded.

Dozens of the original buildings that had been homes and businesses in the 1800s still exist on North Street and in the surrounding neighborhoods. Today, the area is known as the Old North End, or "ONE." It has a positive vibe and synergy with a mix of cultures, restaurants, businesses and community events and activities.

26

The Pine Street South End

As the northern half of Burlington swelled with growth from lumber milling, steam-driven marble milling and shipping during the late 1800s, the north–south Pine Street corridor came to life. It evolved from a rural area into a thriving industrial and residential neighborhood and would sustain itself as the site of steady growth well into the future.

Almost a century after Ira Allen's first log rafts floated down the Onion River and sailed up Lake Champlain toward Canada, the land south of Maple Street began to bustle with activity. The railroad tracks came from New York City to the Burlington waterfront in 1849 and brought a transportation revolution. Docks on the bay were crowded with ships, and over one thousand workers toiled near the waterfront and in mills by the bay. The filled-in waterfront area was piled with lumber, marble and other products. Burlington businesses needed more space to grow, and the south end of town was still undeveloped and open for business. This created new opportunities for merchants to expand on the busy waterfront.

Lumberman Lawrence Barnes found a new way to get an edge over his competition. He was able to buy inexpensive logs from Ottawa, transport them cheaply down the Richelieu River and mill them into lumber at his mill in Burlington. Next, he would ship it by rail all over New England. Barnes made a fortune. In 1856, at a time when the local economy was tanking, he opened a new lumberyard between the lake and Pine Street and revived a furniture-making operation called the Pioneer Shops after it had burned.

Two years later, a trio of businessmen opened another furniture shop and store on Lakeside Avenue. Other enterprises, such as Kilburn & Gates, already ran successful furniture factories near the bay and needed space to expand their operations and shipping. The Pine Street neighborhood became popular for business and development, away from the crowded bay neighborhood.

By 1870, a rectangular canal basin had been dug out behind what is today the Barge Canal Market. The basin is adjacent to the number 13 near the center of the accompanying map. The basin enabled canal boats to come in off the lake, offload or load lumber or other products and then be on their way to other ports. The railroad drawbridge allowed canal boats with masts easy access to the basin. Lumber companies expanded and continued to flourish and profit. After the Civil War, the lumber demand was insatiable, and Burlington responded. By the 1880s, the Burlington waterfront was shipping out 150 million feet of lumber a year.

In 1873, the E.B. & A.C. Whiting Company began making brush fibers in its Pine Street building. More lumber companies, a planing mill, cotton textile weaving mills and maple sugar and syrup packagers moved into the neighborhood. By 1899, a malted cereal operation had opened on Pine Street. Other manufacturers included makers of kitchen utensils, tools, automobile seats, furniture padding, can openers, wood boxes and venetian blinds, to name a few.

During this era, the industrial and residential growth of Burlington and the world was reliant on coal energy for fuel, manufacturing and heating. The Citizens Coal Company bought land between the canal basin and Pine Street and set up a weigh station. But among the dozens of new, expanding and emerging companies, one would forever tarnish the South End lakefront. In 1908, Burlington Gas Works built a coal gasification plant on the southeast side of the canal basin (now known as the barge canal). Over the years, the company dumped excess quantities of coal tar, fuel oil, cyanide and other toxic waste into the canal. Common practices of the past seem almost incomprehensible and incompatible with Vermont values today. And pollution wasn't the only disconcerting practice of the times.

We know from the visual documentation of photographers such as Lewis Wilkes Hines and Louis L. McAllister that at least some of the workers in the lumberyards and mills were boys as young as twelve, some maybe even younger. Although their photos were taken around 1910 at Champlain Wood Working Manufacturing, Hickok Lumber and Chace Mill on the river, it is known that child labor was common before and after that era in Burlington as well as in other places in America.

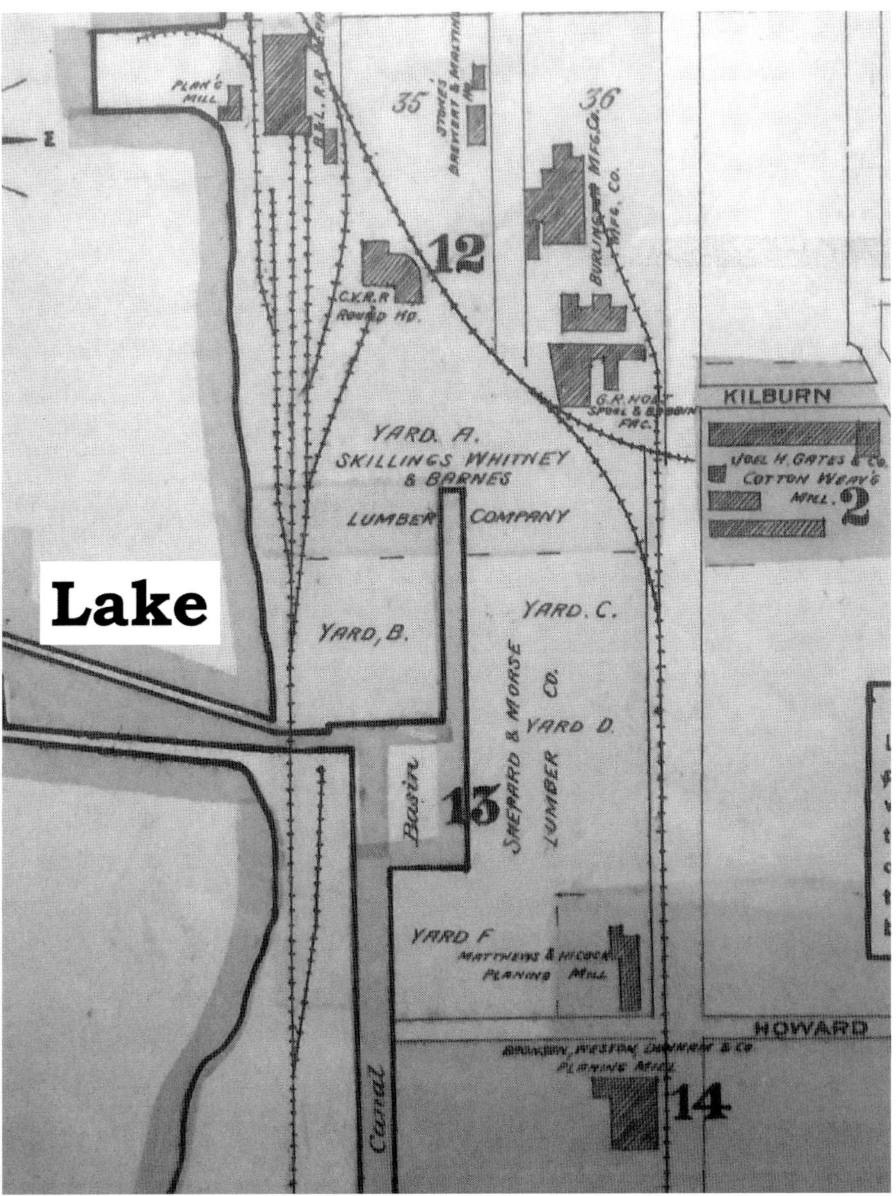

An 1885 Sanborn Insurance map of the Pine Street Lumber Yards and Barge Canal. *Silver Special Collections, UVM.*

As the port and industries grew, there was still plenty of room for expansion in the vast acreage of the South End. The need for workers increased every year, along with the demand for housing, goods, services and churches. St. Anthony's Church was built on the corner of Flynn Avenue and Pine Street for French Canadian workers and their families who labored in the mills and lived in the South End. Landowners and developers saw the demand and profited from subdividing and building neighborhoods in the area.

In 1890, Charles Scarff and A.O. Ferguson bought a large farm and converted it to an eighteen-block residential development between Flynn and Home Avenues. This added to the Lakeside neighborhood that had been built to house the hundreds of textile workers and their families. This acreage, as you might remember, originally adjoined or included William Seward Webb's Oakledge property.

One gem of the South End residential development is the fabled Five Sisters neighborhood, which lies east of Pine Street and west of St. Paul Street. The neighborhood, which includes streets named Caroline, Charlotte, Katherine, Margaret and Marian, as well as Hayward, Ledgemere, Locust and Shelburne, sprouted up in the early 1900s and includes over two hundred single-family homes, duplexes and apartment houses. Caroline, Charlotte and Katherine Streets were named after the daughters of Edward and Maria (Buell) Hungerford. Developer Paul D. Kelley named Margaret and Marian Streets after his wife and a niece, respectively, as the Kelleys had no children. Although the Five Sisters neighborhood might be mistaken for a coherent planned community to the casual observer, it was the product of assorted owners and developers over decades of growth.

Notable architects were involved in the designs of the homes, including Louis S. Newton, John Roberts and William and Ruth Reynolds Freeman. Many of the homes were kit houses that were popular in that era. They were purchased from the Aladdin Company, Gordon–Van Tine Company and Sears, Roebuck & Company. Burlington's 2008 Survey Report of the neighborhood provides a detailed account of that residential neighborhood. The South End and Pine Street in particular have continued to support emerging business and commercial enterprises. Many of the mills have been converted to support emerging needs: housing, software companies, entrepreneurial incubators, restaurants and art studio space, to name a few. There is talk of more commercial and residential development coming to Pine Street soon.

By the time World War I began, most of the Burlington neighborhoods, including the bay, the hill, the large tracts of open land in the urban core,

North Street, the East End and South End had transitioned into a small urban setting. The exception was the far north end of the city on the North Avenue corridor that stretched all the way to the mouth of the river. The New North End, as it is called today, was still largely farmland. Slowly but surely, the New North End experienced residential expansion spurred by twentieth-century factory growth. In the meantime, city officials became increasingly concerned with improving the urban core around Battery Street.

VII

BIG CHANGES IN A SMALL CITY

27

Out with the Old

Longtime Burlington residents remember Bove's Restaurant, one of the last remnants of an Italian neighborhood that existed in the heart of downtown. After closing in 2015, the old restaurant building sits vacant where it operated for seventy years. The building is slated to be a teardown and redeveloped by the Bove family itself, with their hopes for new, larger-scale residential and commercial space.

The author remembers sitting in the Bove's Restaurant back pantry on Sunday afternoons in 1968 with a buddy peeling heaping bowls of garlic cloves and scrubbing pots during lunch for pocket change and a plate of piping hot spaghetti and meatballs. It seemed Bove's spaghetti could be imitated but never equaled, especially considering the ambiance of the old-style booths laid out in three rows and a jukebox, sitting beside the ornate wallpaper under the tall pressed-tin ceilings. The institution outlasted the rest of the Italian businesses, perhaps only because it sat on the north, and not the south, side of Pearl Street.

Despite the treasures of an old-town feel and authentic Italian culinary delights, housing studies in 1915 and 1938 targeted lower Battery Street and the Old North End as areas needing attention. The proximity to Church Street and the potential to capitalize on the spectacular Lake Champlain views gathered steam with developers and merchants. City leaders began to envision suburban shopping centers siphoning away customers and worried about an obsolescent Church Street. The love affair with cars was in full swing, and shoppers wanted better parking and amenities that would also

Two customers at the beauty shop at 40 Pearl Street, near Bove's Restaurant. *Louis Izzo.*

keep the downtown area vital. Re-creating the area west of Church Street seemed like an obvious solution for the city, even at the expense of the urban core neighborhood. Urban renewal was the means to accomplish a goal of a thriving marketplace.

The city wanted to eliminate the neighborhoods in the urban core and make way for modern buildings that would boost the downtown commercial space and tax revenues. The prized twenty-seven-acre rectangular block was bound by Battery, Pearl and College Streets and the east side of Church Street. Proponents of the redevelopment project saw it as an opportunity to remove run-down housing, improve the tax base and take advantage of the million-dollar views of the lake.

In 1959, Burlington voters approved a measure that would permit the city to apply for federal funding for urban renewal. Once the city won the grant, the question of whether Burlington should go through with the proposed urban renewal project was put on the ballot to city residents in March 1962. The voters approved the Urban Renewal Plan with 59 percent of the vote.

Even though it was later referred to as "Little Italy," the neighborhood was equally owned and inhabited by French Canadians, Italians and others. According to city records, of the eighty-eight single- and multi-unit residential properties demolished, there were fifty-four owners in that urban core neighborhood. Of those, fifteen owners were Italian Americans and sixteen were French-Canadian Americans.

Italian and French Canadian families lived, worked, played and worshipped in that area of the city. Where would they go? The answer was to construct new housing for the displaced families on Riverside Avenue and at Fairmont Place off North Avenue. In 1963, the demolition of the old neighborhoods began. The two-story mall was built and attracted commercial success for several decades, until it too became outmoded by new trends.

Hotels, condominiums, offices and small businesses currently populate the area. The Burlington Square Mall, along with malls nationwide, slowly lost business to the convenience and lower prices of online commerce. Today, the city hopes to keep the beautiful, brick-lined marketplace vibrant and healthy, but the city is stalled in another redevelopment project at the mall location. Time will tell the shape of things to come in the urban core.

28

The First Congregational Church Fire

The next few chapters are devoted to architectural monuments that were houses of worship lost to fire in the Queen City over the last two hundred years. Four churches belong to that club, including the First Congregational Church, St. Paul's Episcopal Cathedral, St. Mary's Church and the ensuing Cathedral of the Immaculate Conception.

The formation of the first church in Burlington was complicated by ideology and politics, and this might have ultimately led to its demise. The earliest European settlers in Burlington from Connecticut and Massachusetts were familiar with Calvinist congregations during the Great Awakening, which was a religious revival era. And some of those first Burlington settlers were hoping to revise what they saw as a too-conservative Protestant church and, instead, create a more open-minded, liberal one. This led to two Protestant religious factions in the city, one that was conservative and one that leaned into change.

As part of the original land grant deeds, as a nod to the Church of England, each New Hampshire town grant included acreage set aside for the first settled minister and church. Customarily, the early town leaders looked for candidates to become the clergy of the town church. There were considerable negotiations, disagreements, maneuvers and even dramas surrounding the establishment of Burlington's first church and who would be its first leader. According to some accounts, the two church factions eventually split the church endowment that was established in the town deed. Each faction took half, creating two churches, although this seems to be disputed by the First Unitarian Universalist Society, which says they purchased five acres in 1814 for a second church.

The White Church, aka the First Calvinistic Congregational Church, circa 1820. This building burned and preceded today's First Congregational Church. *First Congregational Church.*

As far back as 1797, 51 of the 2,000 Burlington residents who called themselves the First Society for Social and Public Worship in the Town of Burlington gathered to plan for a house of worship.

It is worth noting that many churches throughout New England had been wrestling with the same ideological struggle: the choice between the more Puritanical conservative status quo versus the more liberal-minded Congregationalists. In a nutshell, Burlington's founders of the first church-to-be became locked in a struggle over whether the new church leader should be a liberal from Harvard or a conservative from Yale. In the end, the nominees for the first minister came down to a Harvard man, Reverend Samuel Clark from Massachusetts, and Reverend Daniel Haskell from Yale in Connecticut.

The disagreement between the camps became palpable and spilled over into the public sphere. A general meeting of Burlington residents (only men could vote, although most church attendees were women) elected the liberal Reverend Clark as minister. When the committee, largely made up of conservatives, failed to change the outcome of the election, it simply nullified Clark as the choice. The conflict between the groups rose to a fever pitch. Church meetings held in the 1802 Burlington Courthouse became contentious to say the least, with palpable animosity and jostling as one group left its meeting and the other group entered the same room for its own meeting. In 1805, a few men and women, led by Daniel Sanders, president of the then-fledgling University of Vermont, signed a covenant establishing the First Calvinist Society of Burlington, Vermont. We should mention Sanders had been educated at Yale and had previously served as the minister of the First Congregational Church in Vergennes.

The congregatin of the conservative Calvinist group raised money and, in 1812, built a white clapboard steepled church on the south side of Pearl Street facing north, the oldest road in the city. The "White Church," as it was known, was near the corner of what is now Pearl Street and South Winooski Avenue. It was initially named the First Calvinist Congregational Church and became a successful gathering place for a congregation.

Not to be outdone, the liberal group proceeded to build their own building, facing south on the north flank of Pearl Street in 1816. They initially named it The First Congregational Society, although it became commonly known as "the red church" or " Brick Meeting House."

A basic street grid had been laid out by William Coit twenty years earlier. The rutted wagon path from Main Street northward to Pearl Street to the red church became a well-traveled route, and the 170-foot-tall steeple, visible the length of the road, anchored the downtown. The modest hodgepodge of residential buildings at the time quickly attracted commercial stores that evolved into the business district of what became known as "Church Street." Both churches coexisted for years, and by 1830, Episcopal and Catholic Churches began stirring in the downtown. Today, the same church at the head of Church Street calls itself The First Unitarian Universalist Society of Burlington. Unfortunately, one of those two churches did not live happily ever after.

At 3:30 a.m. on Sunday, June 23, 1839, the original white Congregational Church bell rang. A fire had started near the belfry area. The bell alerted the engine companies but to no avail. Flames quickly engulfed the steeple, which raged and devoured the heavy beams that crashed down through the roof into the sanctuary. The building quickly burned to the ground. It had been recently renovated and included an expensive organ. None of it

An 1835 image of the Red Church, aka the Brick Church, aka The First Congregational Society, at the head of Church Street. *Silver Special Collections, UVM.*

was insured. A $1,000 reward was offered for information leading to the supposed arsonist. The January 17, 1840 *Burlington Weekly Free Press* reported that a man pleaded guilty to setting the fire, and he was later sentenced to five years in prison, much to the dismay of the newspaper reporter, who likened burning the church to "burning the town."

Within a few years, a new brick First Congregational Church was built on the same property next to South Winooski Avenue facing Cherry Street. The 1840s building is adorned with a distinctive columned Greek Revival tower instead of a traditional pointed steeple. It still stands today, reassuringly visible from Church Street. Eventually, the First Congregational Church and The First Unitarian Universalist Society mended their ways, and each found a significant place of importance in the community.

29

The St. Paul's Episcopal Cathedral Fire

St. Paul's Church was organized by a group of over fifty Burlington Episcopalians in 1830. This was a time when Burlington's working-class population, living in the urban core area between Battery and Church Streets, was expanding. Early church services were held in the courthouse before the building was finished.

In 1831, the Right Reverend John Henry Hopkins was appointed Episcopal Bishop of Vermont. Hopkins carried on a bitter dogmatic and sometimes personal feud with the Catholic reverend Jeremiah O'Callaghan, about whom we will learn more later. Hopkins was active in building the Episcopalian community and started a boys' school at about the same time.

In 1832, the neo-Gothic limestone church was dedicated. As the congregation grew, the building expanded with several renovations in 1851, 1866 and again after a small fire in 1910. St. Paul's Episcopal Church experienced significant growth during the twentieth century and in 1965 was designated the Cathedral Church of the Episcopalian Diocese. A cathedral is defined as being recognized as a larger church and is run by a bishop, not by a priest.

As mentioned previously, the places of worship were essential to the early families of newcomers who built much of the early city and, later on, to those who lived in the urban core that surrounded the church. St. Paul's was centrally located, anchored in the middle of the working-class residential district of Burlington Bay.

St. Paul's Episcopal Cathedral on St. Paul Street, undated. *Silver Special Collections, UVM.*

After serving the community for 140 years, on February 16, 1971, St. Paul's Cathedral was set ablaze, the result of an electrical problem. According to newspaper accounts, the intensity of the fire updraft launched flaming hymnal pages into the air, later to float back down to earth miles up the hill on the UVM green. The cathedral had been built just a block from the Baptist church on St. Paul Street, which survives today.

The timing of the fire was impeccable: It happened in the midst of Burlington's urban renewal project, which relocated the residential neighborhoods out of that area in favor of a city-planned commercial mall. As tragic as the fire was for parishioners and the city, it presented an opportunity for the city's redevelopment plans. Having been located in the heart of downtown, the city proposed a land swap to rebuild the cathedral a couple of blocks away, on a lot nearer the lake with westerly views. This would facilitate the city to use the former property.

The congregation regrouped and negotiated the land swap. The large lot on the corner of Pearl and Battery Streets would serve as an alternative site for the new cathedral. The controversial and contentious decision resulted in the Burlington Square Mall and parking garage being built on

St. Paul's Episcopal Cathedral interior, St. Paul Street, undated. *Silver Special Collections, UVM.*

or near the site of the old cathedral. The new cathedral and congregation kept to their mission and built an affordable, multi-unit residence for older adults on their new property known as Cathedral Square. The residence adjoins the new, modern cathedral. Eight of the original nine bells still toll in the new bell tower.

Incidentally, as this is written, the property of the original cathedral is the site of modern apartment housing and commercial space. Adjacent is a deep, several-years-old construction crater waiting for work to proceed on a project that has been designed to keep the Church Street Marketplace viable for another generation. The new residential/commercial project, called CityPlace, will come to fruition in several years' time if the gods are willing.

30

St. Mary's and the Cathedral of the Immaculate Conception Fires

The Roman Catholic church in Burlington started out with humble beginnings as St. Mary's Church in 1830, located on a bluff of land that is now a cemetery at the junction of Hyde Street and Riverside Avenue. The small wood church established and built in 1832 by the combative and controversial Irish-born Father Jeremiah O'Callaghan didn't last long. On May 11, 1838, while O'Callaghan was out of town, it burned down. Since there was no electricity or fire going in the church, the cause was believed to be arson.

Allegations and conspiracy theories ensued, especially as it preceded the Congregational Church fire on Pearl Street that occurred a year later. However polarizing he had been, Father O'Callaghan persuasively raised money from Catholics and Protestants alike to build a new church, this time on the southeast corner of Cherry and St. Paul Streets, in the heart of the Irish neighborhoods and the French-speaking neighborhoods to the north.

A new St. Mary's church building was underway in 1841. The construction commenced before the Civil War but was not completed to the point that the building could be used for services until 1867. Much of the red stone in the Gothic building was quarried in Burlington at Willard's quarry, east of Shelburne Street, and black marble limestone came from a quarry in Isle La Motte. The interior Gothic pillars came from a West Rutland marble quarry. The bodies of the Bishops Louis DeGosbriand, John Stephen Michaud, Joseph John Rice and Edward Francis Ryan were buried in a crypt beneath the door of the cathedral.

The Cathedral of the Immaculate Conception. *Detroit Publishing Co., 1900, Library of Congress.*

The awe-inspiring cathedral was finally completed in 1904 and topped with a commissioned fourteen-foot-tall vulcanized copper and gold-leaf statue of Our Lady of Lourdes from France. During renovations, the original bell, which had cracked, was replaced with a new 4,500-pound bell in 1960. The beautiful stained-glass windows, shrines and unique stations of the cross were magnificent highlights for many visitors from within and outside the Catholic faith.

The Cathedral of the Immaculate Conception interior, 1938. *Kathleen Messier, Archives of the Roman Catholic Diocese of Burlington.*

To many, the cathedral was the most architecturally impressive of the lost churches. It burned at the hands of an arsonist on March 13, 1972. In the early stages of the cathedral fire on that fateful night, neighbors and bar patrons from nearby establishments helped firemen unload and man water hoses before mutual aid arrived from Winooski, South Burlington, Essex, Malletts Bay, Colchester, Shelburne and the Burlington Auxiliary departments. Not long after midnight, during the raging inferno, the bell tower collapsed. The building and all of its treasures were lost.

The arsonist confessed to setting the fire and was found to be insane and was admitted to the state hospital. To make matters worse, the city was living on the edge through that dark time. During the previous year and in the months after the fire, other arsonists had set fire to the Mayfair store on Church Street, burned down the Strong Block on Main Street, an entire block on North Street and eight buildings within the North Street and Elmwood Avenue neighborhood, not to mention the shock of the St. Paul's Cathedral fire the year before.

Our Lady of Lourdes, the fourteen-foot-tall vulcanized copper, gold-leaf statue commissioned from France. It stood atop the Cathedral of the Immaculate Conception until the church burned in 1971. The statue now looks out over St. Anne's Shrine, Isle La Motte, Vermont. *Courtesy of the author.*

The cathedral was rebuilt with a more modern design near the same site. But over the years, attendance declined and urban renewal relocated some of the residential neighborhoods away from the area. St. Joseph's Church on Allen Street, a few blocks away, became a co-cathedral, and today the rebuilt modern Cathedral of the Immaculate Conception is empty and for sale. The two-ton bell rests high on metal support beams at the location of the original steeple near Cherry Street. The captivating gold statue of Our Lady of Lourdes, which survived the fire, was given new life at Vermont's oldest European religious site, dating back to the 1600s, at St. Anne's Shrine in Isle La Motte.

31

Sheltering in Place

Although joking about taxes putting us "in the poorhouse" is a common expression, in the old days, the poorhouse was no laughing matter. Even in a small city like Burlington, a growing number of people found themselves in need of shelter. Homelessness increased during times of stress, such as the Irish Potato Famine, the return to civilian life of men with disabilities from the American Revolution and the Civil War, economic hardships and scares, the outbreaks of diseases, surges in mental illness and other life-changing events. Another contributing factor was the status of people in poor health and destitution in old age before the advent of mental health treatment, Social Security and other social programs. Moreover, as the general population grew, the number of people unable to support themselves also increased across Vermont and the country. Some people were seasonally transient; others needed permanent shelter and food.

Some believed it was in the towns' best interests to reduce their local responsibilities for supporting impoverished transients. This led towns to define who qualified as actual residents and who unduly wanted to take advantage of town services. In the late 1700s, towns began "warning out" individuals who were found to be unwelcome. "Warning out" involved escorting persons to the edge of town and officially sending them on their way. This helped rid a town of wanderers but sent them into neighboring towns, resurfacing somewhere else.

In response to a growing population of individuals who were physically disabled, mentally ill, old, infirm or otherwise unable to support themselves, the state stepped in. The Vermont legislature passed a relief act in 1797, known as "An Act for relieving and ordering Idiots; Impotent, Distracted and Idle Persons." In some cases, families were unable or too poor to care for their loved ones with mental illness or developmental challenges. These persons became the responsibility of the town. According to the *Journal of the Vermont Historical Society*, the legislation also required each community to prevent the poor from alternatively strolling into any other towns as well.

Paupers were sometimes accommodated by families willing to take responsibility for them with very little or no compensation. Others, including the mentally ill, were placed in almshouses, poor farms, workhouses or jails. And there were cases of abuse. In Hartford, Vermont, one insane "inmate," as he was called, was confined to a metal cage at its poor farm in 1832. The Vermont Asylum for the Insane was not opened until 1834.

In fact, in the early 1800s, most towns in Vermont had created their own poor farms to support those who couldn't support themselves. But at that time, public thinking in the state had not caught up with emerging beliefs from the medical community that insanity was a medical illness that could be treated. In order to solve these problems and provide support to towns, poor farms and poorhouses sprouted up around the state and throughout New England in the early 1800s, before the establishment of the Vermont asylum. Before long, the poor farms and houses, which in some cases were a throwback to the way things were done as far back as the 1600s in Europe, were common all over New England.

The farm residents included men, women and children "inmates" and were managed by an "overseer," who was often the lowest bidder in each town. In some cases, farmers offered their existing farms for use as poor farms; in other cases, towns leased, purchased or built their own properties to use. The "inmates" of the farms included individual men and women, as well as entire families. Men and women were fed and housed separately. Those who were able to work did so on the farms. Those who could not work often lived out their years there.

In Burlington, one of the earliest mentions of caring for the poor dates to 1816, when a building in the Battery Park military base, most likely the hospital, was leased by the city for use as a poor farm. And Burlington, which was still a town until 1865, leased several locations during the first few decades. In 1824, the town bought a building at the southwest corner of South Union and College Streets, at the site of the present-day College Street Congregational Church. In 1836, the town purchased the Purdy farm on the west side of Shelburne Road at the present junction of I-89, and it was used as a poor farm for many years. The farm was apparently replaced with a brick building that could hold as many as seventy-five residents.

Many years' worth of Burlington's "Poor Department" and "Overseer of the Poor" receipts and ledgers chronicle the expenditures, dating to the 1800s. One crude sketch by Burlington architect John Johnson in 1838, apparently for the Shelburne Road farm, shows the layout of the building. It includes walls, chimneys and stoves for a two-story building. Receipts from the 1840s and 1850s show purchases of lamp oil, codfish, coffee, tobacco, a spitoon, furniture, bedding, material for sheets and pillowcases, kitchen utensils, cordwood and medicines, as well as records of doctor's appointments. The records paint a picture of an organization that housed dozens of people, some for short tenures and others permanently.

The very thorough 1866 records detail the purchase of dozens of farming tools, human and horse medicines, the use of a hearse and probate costs. That year, detailed records indicate the number of people who resided at the poor house (16 adults and 13 children), the number of different people who resided during the year (106) and those who were helped outside of the house (146). The records show charges for several adult coffins, child coffins and grave-digging. It was noted that a man and a woman died at the house during that year, and seven died outside the house, for which the city paid burial expenses.

By the late 1800s, Burlington was using the services of other institutions to help treat the poorhouse residents. The overseer folder includes an 1876 invoice from the Brattleboro Asylum for the Insane for "support" of a dozen named patients. One column includes numbers that might represent time intervals in weeks. Several patients have "52" entered, and one has "12 4/7." This might reflect a twelve-week and four-day stay at the asylum, which was noted for its high-quality and humane treatments, including relaxing water baths, fitness programs, crafts, music and community programs. The invoice shows a payable amount of $156.00 due for each of the patients listed at "52." The subtotal cost for the twelve patients is $1,109.15, with additional subtotals added for mileage and state aid.

The records also show a trail of invoices for services to individuals and families residing outside the poorhouse. These include everything from doctors' appointments to medicine and food. But a new improvement would come during the Civil War era.

During the 1860s, a young Burlington girl, whose parents were jailed, was sent to the Burlington Poor Farm. Recognizing that the facility wasn't the ideal nurturing environment for a girl without a family, a local woman named Lucia Wheeler found the girl a good adoptive home. Over the course of a few years, Wheeler did the same for seven other girls and was able to bring together a few other women to raise money for a new home for children who needed safe places to live. As a result, the Home for Destitute Children was established on the corner of Home Avenue and Shelburne Road in 1865. In fact, Home Avenue derived its name from the facility. Records appear to show the house to have operated solely on donations of cash, food and sundries.

In 1893, the home burned. Miraculously, all seventy-one residents survived. A large brick building was erected to serve as the new home, which continued to be successful. Several benefactors, including John Purple Howard and David Baird from New York City donated substantial funding. It was renamed the Children's Home and was subsequently moved to Pine Street and later became the Josephine Baird Children's Center, in honor of David Baird's beloved wife.

Everything seemed to be going smoothly for the poor farm on Shelburne Road until 1896, when the overseer of the poor noted inadequacies at the farm. The city sold the Shelburne Road property. Within a few decades, the old poor farm location would become a retail shopping center on the site where Home Goods, TJ Maxx, Price Chopper and Buffalo Wild Wings are located today.

The last Burlington Poor House on Goodrich Road, at the site of C.P. Smith School on Ethan Allen Parkway today. *1957 City of Burlington Annual Report.*

In 1904, the city purchased the Goodrich farm on Goodrich Road (now known as Ethan Allen Parkway) off North Avenue in the New North End. The brick residential building, a barn, an abandoned building and sheds sat on fifty-four acres. Gardens managed by the caretaker, his wife and some residents supplied all of the food needs for the residents. The building had formerly served as an isolated smallpox hospital, and apparently, the north wing had been built on a budget by the WPA. As a result, that newer wing could never be heated properly, and it was believed that renovations would outprice a new building.

A 1955 *Burlington Free Press* cover story reported that city aldermen were weighing the demolition of the aging building, selling off some adjoining land and rolling the profits into a modern nursing home. They saw the move as a way to save money, but were also mindful of changing practices in care. They noted that Burlington was one of only a handful of towns with still-operating poor farms in Vermont.

The Goodrich Road location existed until 1957, when the building was demolished and C.P. Smith School was built on the site. At the time, newspaper articles noted that voters approved money for a nursing home, which was being promoted by the city's welfare commission.

Burlington, like other cities, has developed community mental health services, residences for older people, nursing homes, homeless shelters and advocacy programs that are sometimes funded by philanthropists and run by nonprofits. Some are city-funded, others find state or federal government funding and some are for-profit. But as in most other cities, not all of the homeless have adequate shelter, food and wellbeing. But the records show that as far back as the early 1800s, the people of Burlington were dedicated to providing food, care and shelter to those who could not care for themselves, and services have improved over time.

Bibliography

Anonymous [Nathaniel Hawthorne]. "The Inland Port," *New-England Magazine*, no. 9 (December 1835): 398–409.

"Art Cohn: The Sinking of the General Butler" (video transcript). University of Vermont, College of Arts and Sciences, Burlington, Vermont, 2021. https:www.uvm.edu.

Bachellor, Albert S. *The New Hampshire Grants: Begin Transcripts of The Charters of Townships And Minor Grants of Lands Made By The Provincial Government of New Hampshire, Within the Present Boundaries of The State of Vermont, From 1749 to 1764.* Concord, NH: Edward N. Pearson, 1895.

Baird, Joel Banner. "What Lies Beneath Burlington?" *Burlington Free Press*, June 30, 2014.

Barmak, Sarah. "John Dewey: Education's Charles Darwin." *Toronto Star*, October 25, 2009.

Beach, Bob, Jr. Personal interview by email, October 25, 2021.

Blanchard, Robert. "Burlington Poor Farms." Burlington Area History Facebook Page, October 24, 2019. http://www.facebook.com.

———. "Phineas Loomis." Burlington Area History Facebook Page, June 13, 2021. https://www.facebook.com.

———. "Steamboats." Burlington Area History Facebook Page, June 22, 2021. https://www.facebook.com.

Blow, David J. *Historic Guide to Burlington Neighborhoods*. Chittenden County Historical Society, 1990.

———. Personal interviews by email. July–December 2021.

Bourgerie, Gabrielle. "University of Vermont." *UVM National Register North Street Burlington Vermont Statement of Significance*. University of Vermont, Burlington, Vermont, April 1996. http://www.uvm.edu.

Burlington 1830. "Introduction." UVM Historic Preservation Program. Burlington, Vermont, n.d. http://www.uvm.edu.

"Burlington, Vermont Early 20th-Century Postcard Views." HP 206 Researching Historic Structures & Sites. UVM Historic Preservation Program, 2012. http://www.uvm.edu.

Burlington Free Press. "City May Close Poor Farm." September 27, 1955, 1.

Burlington Geographic. "Landscape Lenses." N.d. http://place.w3.uvm.edu.

Burlington Weekly Free Press. "Tales of the Sea: James Wakefield's Interesting Experiences of Sixty Years Ago." December 16, 1909, 9.

Bushnell, Mark. "Care, Sometimes Abuse on Vermont's Poor Farms." VTDigger, January 19, 2020. https://vtdigger.org.

———. "Then Again: Betting on the Wrong Iron Horse." VTDigger, September 17, 2017. https://vtdigger.org.

Carlisle, Lilian Baker. "Humanities' Needs Deserve Our Fortune: Mary Martha Fletcher and the Fletcher Family Benevolences." *Vermont History Journal* (1982). https://vermonthistory.org.

Cathedral Church of St. Paul. "History: About St. Paul's Cathedral." https://www.stpaulscathedralvt.org.

City of Burlington. "Vermont War of 1812 Sites: Battery Street Area." American Battlefield Protection Program. USDOI, NPS, City of Burlington, GA 2255-10-003, n.d.

———. "Vermont War of 1812 Sites: Downtown Area." American Battlefield Protection Program. USDOI, NPS, City of Burlington, GA 2255-10-003, n.d.

———. "Vermont War of 1812 Sites: Military Cantonment and Soldiers' Burial Ground." American Battlefield Protection Program. USDOI, NPS, City of Burlington, n.d.

———. "Vermont War of 1812 Sites: University of Vermont Green." American Battlefield Protection Program. USDOI, NPS, City of Burlington, GA 2255-10-003, n.d.

City of Burlington Planning Office. "City of Burlington Urban Renewal Agency Property Records: Champlain Street Urban Renewal Project, 1963." Burlington, Vermont.

Cohn, Arthur B. *Lake Champlain's Sailing Canal Boats: An Illustrated Journey from Burlington Bay to the Hudson River*. Lake Champlain Maritime Museum, 2003.

Cohn, Arthur B., and Kevin J. Crisman. *When Horses Walked on Water*. Washington, DC: Smithsonian Institution Press, 1998.

Colman, Devin. "Burlington Survey of the Five Sisters Neighborhood." *Survey Report*. Burlington, Vermont, October 15, 2008. https://www.burlingtonvt.gov.

"The Converse Home." 272 Church Street, Burlington 1830. UVM Historic Preservation Program, Burlington, Vermont, N.d. http://www.uvm.edu.

Czaikowski, Karen. Mill St., Burlington. Division of Historic Preservation. https://www2.burlingtonvt.gov.

DeSeife, Ethan. "An Engineer and Map Geek Unearths Burlington's Past." *Seven Days*, December 23, 2014.

Dykhuizen, George. *Journal of the History of Ideas* (December 1959).
———. *The Life and Mind of John Dewey*. Carbondale: Southern Illinois University Press, 1978.
"FAQs: Vermont Italian Cultural Association." *Vermont Italian Cultural Association* (2021). https://www.vermontitalianculturalassociation.org.
Fay, Glenn. *Vermont's Ebenezer Allen: Patriot, Commando and Emancipator*. Charleston, SC: Arcadia Publishing, 2021.
Feeney, Vincent E. *Burlington: A History of Vermont's Queen City*. Bennington, VT: Images from the Past, 2015.
———. "Pre-Famine Irish in Vermont, 1815–1844." *Vermont Historical Society Journal* 74 (Summer/Fall 2006): 101–26.
Feeney, Vincent, and Brendan Keleher. "Burlington's Ethnic Communities, 1860–1900." *Vermont Historical Society Journal* 86 (2018).
———. "Burlington's Historic Urban Core: Evolution of Neighborhood." *Bulletin* 50, no. 1 (Winter 2021). Chittenden County Historical Society.
First Unitarian Universalist Society of Burlington. "Our History." 2021. https://uusociety.org/information/history.
"Focal Places in Burlington," *Burlington Geographic*. PLACE: Place-Based Landscape Analysis and Community Engagement. University of Vermont, n.d. http://www.uvm.edu.
Gillen, Mollie. *The Prince and His Lady: The Love Story of the Duke of Kent and Madame de St. Laurent*. Halifax, Nova Scotia: Formac Publishing, 2005.
"Greensboro Bend: The Abenaki People," PLACE: Place-Based Landscape Analysis and Community Engagement. University of Vermont, n.d. https://www.uvm.edu.
Grey, Julia. "Retrospective Burlington: Case Studies in Preservation." Community Preservation Projects in Burlington, n.d. http://www.uvm.edu.
Hapner, Christopher. "Fire Destroys Catholic Cathedral." *Burlington Free Press*, March 14, 1972.
Haswell MSS, Special Collections, University of Vermont, District of Vermont, Customs Office. January 19, 1808.
Hebert, Christine Auer. Personal interview by phone, October 21, 2021.
Higbee, William Wallace. *Around the Mountains*. Copy of the original manuscript, Special Collections, UVM, 28.
Hoffbeck, Steven R. "'Remember the Poor': (Galatians 2:10) Poor Farms in Vermont." *Journal of the Vermont Historical Society* (Fall 1989).
Johnson, Michael. Pearl House, Burlington 1830, UVM Historic Preservation Program, n.d. http://www.uvm.edu.
Jones, David W. "Moral Insanity and Psychological Disorder: The Hybrid Roots of Psychiatry." *History of Psychiatry*. Thousand Oaks, CA: SAGE Publications, 2017. https://www.ncbi.nlm.nih.gov.
Kelley, Kevin J. "Lost and Found: Signs Reclaim Burlington's Historic 'Little Italy' Neighborhood." *Seven Days*, January 14, 2021. https://www.sevendaysvt.com.
King, Liz. "Retrospective Burlington: Case Studies in Preservation." UVM Historic Preservation Program, n.d., http://www.uvm.edu.

Kirkness, Elizabeth. "Century of Children…." *Burlington Free Press*, October 25, 1965.

Kung, Steven. "Burlington Traction Company Records." *Vermont Historical Society* (July 2011). https://vermonthistory.org.

Lake Champlain Maritime Museum. "Shipwrecks: Sailing Canal Boat *General Butler*." 2021. https://www.lcmm.org.

Lincoln, Howard. Personal interview. Donor Relations and Stewardship, UVM Foundation, November 11, 2021.

Livi, Andrea. "342 Pearl Street: Klifa House, Burlington 1830." University of Vermont Historic Preservation Program, Burlington, Vermont, n.d. http://www.uvm.edu.

McGovern, Constance M. "The Insane, the Asylum, and the State, in Nineteenth-Century Vermont." *Vermont Historical Society Journal* (1984). https://vermonthistory.org.

Muller, H.N. "Smuggling into Canada: How the Champlain Valley Defied Jefferson's Embargo." *Vermont Historical Society Journal* (1970). https://vermonthistory.org.

Norwood, Karyn. "Mills & Factories." *From Cereal to Can Openers: Historic Industries along Pine Street—By Karyn Norwood*. UVM Historic Preservation Program, Burlington, Vermont, 2014. https://www.uvm.edu.

O'Callaghan, E.B. *The Documentary History of the State of New York: Arranged by Hon. Christopher Horan, Secretary of State*. Vol. 2. Albany, NY: Weed, Parsons & Co., 1849.

O'Neil, Daniel. "Uncoiling the Black Snake Affair." *Burlington Free Press*, September 25, 2014.

O'Neil, Mary. "The Gideon King House." *Burlington 1830*, University of Vermont, n.d., http://www.uvm.edu.

Peabody, G. Donald. *From the East, Bearing Gifts: Vermont's Firsts to the Nation*. N.p.: Vermont Books Press, 2013.

Porter, Doug. "166-Battery, Pomeroy House, Burlington 1830." University of Vermont Historic Preservation Program, Burlington, Vermont, n.d. http://www.uvm.edu.

Potash, Jeff. Email conversation, December 15, 2021.

Provost, David. "A Gem of Architecture: The History of Billings Library." UVM Historic Preservation Program, December 2, 1999. http://www.uvm.edu.

Ramsey, Connie Cain. "The Black Snake Affair." Courthouse Chronicle #7. https://static1.squarespace.com.

Rann, William S. *The History of Chittenden County with Illustrations and Biographical Sketches*. Syracuse, NY: D. Mason & Company, 1886.

Reimann, Liisa. "Fletcher Allen Health Care." *Historic Burlington*. Burlington: University of Vermont, 2004. http://www.uvm.edu.

"Rutland Railroad Archive," Middlebury College Archives, Davis Family Library Special Collections, Identifier C-117. https://archivesspace.middlebury.edu.

Silberman, Alexandre, and Cerella Farinholt. "Into the Archives: A Look at the *Register*'s Historic Past." *BHS Register*. Burlington High School, April 30, 2017. https://bhsregister.com.

Spaulding, Albert C. "Trolleys." *Vermont Life* (Spring 1964).

Stone, Arthur F. *The Vermont of Today*. Vol. 4. New York: Lewis Historical Publishing Co, 1929.

Thomas, John D. *The University of Vermont*. Charleston, SC: Arcadia Publishing, 2006.

United States Army Corps of Engineers. *List of Bridges over the Navigable Waters of the United States*. Washington, DC: U.S. Government Printing Office, 1936.

Vermont Asylum for the Insane: Its Annals for Fifty Years. Brattleboro, VT: Hildreth & Fales, 1887.

Vermont Judiciary. "The History of the Vermont Judiciary." n.d. https://www.vermontjudiciary.org.

Visser, Thomas. "Billings Student Center," University of Vermont, 1999. http:///www.uvm.edu.

———. "The Old Mill," University of Vermont, 1998. http://www.uvm.edu.

Wayside Exhibits, Oakledge Park, Governor's Institute and Lake Champlain Basin Program, 2003.

Woodsmoke Productions and Vermont Historical Society. "The Age of Trolleys, 1901." *Green Mountain Chronicles* radio broadcast, original broadcast 1988–89. https://vermonthistory.org.

About the Author

Glenn Fay Jr. is a seventh-generation Vermonter and a descendant of Daniel Champion, a Green Mountain Boy who served in Warner's Regiment during the Revolutionary War. Glenn grew up in and has lived in Burlington much of his life, and graduated from the University of Vermont with advanced degrees. He taught high school science and worked as an adjunct professor at UVM for many years. His first book, *Vermont's Ebenezer Allen: Patriot, Commando and Emancipator*, is the biography of a Green Mountain Boy who was the first Vermonter to publicly emancipate an enslaved woman and her infant daughter. Glenn is an avid historian and serves on the board of directors at the Ethan Allen Homestead Museum.